→

THE SWISS INSTITUTE – CONTEMPORARY ART GRATEFULLY
ACKNOWLEDGES THE PARTNERSHIP AND SUPPORT OF THE
FOLLOWING CONTRIBUTORS, WHOSE COMMITMENT ENABLED
BOTH THE GROUP EXHIBITION AND THE BOOK **EXTRA**:

SWISSPEAKS*FESTIVAL*, NEW YORK
PRO HELVETIA (ARTS COUNCIL OF SWITZERLAND)
PRS PRESENCE SWITZERLAND
SWISS INTERNATIONAL AIR LINES
ÉTANT DONNÉS, PARIS
STANLEY THOMAS JOHNSON FOUNDATION
CULTURAL SERVICES OF THE FRENCH EMBASSY, NEW YORK
CHRISTOPH MERIAN VERLAG, BASEL
CLIFF DIVER
TRANSCONTAINER TRANSPORT, INC.
SWISS WORLD CARGO

THE S I WOULD LIKE TO THANK THE FOLLOWING GALLERIES
AND INSTITUTIONS FOR THEIR HELPFUL COOPERATION
WITH THE GROUP EXHIBITION **EXTRA**:

FRAC BOURGOGNE, DIJON
GALERIE LOEVENBRUCK, PARIS
GALERIE THADDEAUS ROPAC, PARIS
SONNABEND GALLERY, NEW YORK
SPERONE WESTWATER GALLERY, NEW YORK

THE S I WOULD ALSO LIKE TO THANK EVERYONE
LISTED ON THE PAGES 434 – 438

HOW MANY EXTRA LAYERS CAN WE GRAFT ONTO REALITY
BEFORE IT COLLAPSES?

UM WIEVIELE EXTRA-SCHICHTEN KÖNNEN WIR DIE REALITÄT
ERWEITERN BEVOR SIE ZUSAMMENBRICHT?

PUBLISHED ON THE OCCASION OF THE GROUP EXHIBITION
EXTRA AT THE SWISS INSTITUTE – CONTEMPORARY ART,
NEW YORK, MARCH 5 – APRIL 26, 2003.

ERSCHIENEN ANLÄSSLICH DER GRUPPENAUSSTELLUNG
EXTRA IM SWISS INSTITUTE – CONTEMPORARY ART,
NEW YORK, 5. MÄRZ – 26. APRIL 2003.

VISUAL ESSAYS / BILDBEITRÄGE
VIRGINIE BARRÉ, OLIVIER BLANCKART, OLAF BREUNING,
STÉPHANE DAFFLON, WIM DELVOYE, PETER FISCHLI /
DAVID WEISS, SYLVIE FLEURY, DANIEL FIRMAN, GELATIN,
JANINE GORDON, FABRICE GYGI, LORI HERSBERGER,
CHRISTIAN JANKOWSKI, JUTTA KOETHER / STEVEN PARRINO ,
OLIVIER MOSSET, GIANNI MOTTI, ERIK PARKER,
BRUNO PEINADO, UGO RONDINONE / JOHN GIORNO /
URS FISCHER, JEAN-CLAUDE RUGGIRELLO,
STÉPHANE SAUTOUR, JIM SHAW, ROMAN SIGNER,
OLAV WESTPHALEN, ERWIN WURM

TEXTS / TEXTE
DAVID DEUTSCH (CENTRE FOR QUANTUM COMPUTATION,
OXFORD) / SETH LLOYD (MASSACHUSETTS INSTITUTE
OF TECHNOLOGY), BOB NICKAS, MARTIN TUPPER,
MARC-OLIVIER WAHLER

EDITOR AND CURATOR / HERAUSGEBER UND KURATOR
MARC-OLIVIER WAHLER

PUBLISHER / VERLEGER
SWISS INSTITUTE – CONTEMPORARY ART, NEW YORK

CO-PUBLISHER / KO-VERLEGER
CHRISTOPH MERIAN VERLAG

PUBLISHER / VERLEGER

SWISS INSTITUTE - CONTEMPORARY ART
495 BROADWAY 3RD FLOOR
NEW YORK NY 10012
WWW.SWISSINSTITUTE.NET

CO-PUBLISHER / KO-VERLEGER

CHRISTOPH MERIAN VERLAG
ST. ALBAN-VORSTADT 5
4002 BASEL SWITZERLAND
WWW.CHRISTOPH-MERIAN-VERLAG.CH

DISTRIBUTION / VERTRIEB USA, CDN:
D.A.P./ DISTRIBUTED ART PUBLISHERS
155 SIXTH AVENUE, NEW YORK, NY 10013
WWW.ARTBOOK.COM

FOR ALL OTHER COUNTRIES:
ISBN 3-85616-191-0
CHRISTOPH MERIAN VERLAG

PUBLISHED AT THE OCCASION OF THE GROUP EXHIBITION
EXTRA AT SWISS INSTITUTE - CONTEMPORARY ART,
NEW YORK MARCH 5 - APRIL 26, 2003

ERSCHIENEN ANLÄSSLICH DER GRUPPENAUSSTELLUNG
EXTRA IM SWISS INSTITUTE - CONTEMPORARY ART,
NEW YORK, 5. MÄRZ - 26. APRIL 2003

EDITOR / HERAUSGEBER

MARC-OLIVIER WAHLER

CONTRIBUTORS / MITWIRKENDE

VIRGINIE BARRÉ, OLIVIER BLANCKART, OLAF BREUNING,
STÉPHANE DAFFLON, WIM DELVOYE, DAVID DEUTSCH
(CENTRE FOR QUANTUM COMPUTATION, OXFORD),
DANIEL FIRMAN, URS FISCHER, PETER FISCHLI /
DAVID WEISS, SYLVIE FLEURY, GELATIN, JOHN GIORNO,
JANINE GORDON, FABRICE GYGI, LORI HERSBERGER,
CHRISTIAN JANKOWSKI, JUTTA KOETHER, SETH LLOYD
(MIT CAMBRIDGE), OLIVIER MOSSET, GIANNI MOTTI,
BOB NICKAS, ERIK PARKER, STEVEN PARRINO, BRUNO
PEINADO, UGO RONDINONE, JEAN-CLAUDE RUGGIRELLO,
STÉPHANE SAUTOUR, JIM SHAW, ROMAN SIGNER,
MARTIN TUPPER, MARC-OLIVIÉR WAHLER, OLAV
WESTPHALEN AND ERWIN WURM

TRANSLATION / ÜBERSETZUNG

STÉPHANE BARMANN, GABRIELLE GIATTINO

PROOF-READING / LEKTORAT

JEAN-CHRISTOPHE BLASER, KRISTIN JONES,
CARMEN PENNELLA, EVELINE STEINMANN,
DAN TIERNEY, IRIS MEDER

GRAPHIC DESIGN / GESTALTUNG

NIKLAUS THÖNEN, WIEN
WITH THE HELP OF MAIA GUSBERTI, TINA HOCHKOGLER

SCANS / LITHOS

NIKLAUS THÖNEN, WIEN
WITH THE HELP OF KARL ULBL

PAPER / PAPIER

BIBERIST FURIOSO 135 / 90 G/M^2

TYPEFACE / SCHRIFT

BLENDER (RE-P.)

PRINTED BY / DRUCK

GUGLER PRINT & MEDIA, MELK
PRINTED IN AUSTRIA

PRINTED IN COMPLIANCE WITH INTERNATIONAL
ENVIRONMENTAL PRINTING REGULATIONS

GEDRUCKT NACH DEN RICHTLINIEN
SCHADSTOFFARME DRUCKERZEUGNISSE

BIBLIOGRAPHIC INFORMATION PUBLISHED BY DIE
DEUTSCHE BIBLIOTHEK: DIE DEUTSCHE BIBLIOTHEK
LISTS THIS PUBLICATION IN THE DEUTSCHE
NATIONALBIBLIOGRAFIE; DETAILED BIBLIOGRAPHIC DATA
IS AVAILABLE IN THE INTERNET AT HTTP://DNB.DDB.DE.

BIBLIOGRAFISCHE INFORMATION DER DEUTSCHEN
BIBLIOTHEK: DIE DEUTSCHE BIBLIOTHEK VERZEICHNET
DIESE PUBLIKATION IN DER DEUTSCHEN
NATIONALBIBLIOGRAFIE; DETAILLIERTE BIBLIOGRAFISCHE
DATEN SIND IM INTERNET ÜBER HTTP://DNB.DDB.DE
ABRUFBAR.

S I

SWISS INSTITUTE – CONTEMPORARY ART, NEW YORK

The SI is very pleased to organize the group show EXTRA and to publish this accompanying book. Both are a testimony to this institution's unique angle, which fosters the interaction between the Swiss and the many other communities and nationalities present in New York City. The program of the past years has been an evolution toward becoming an innovative, international venue for young contemporary art and toward a way of thinking that asks audiences to look beyond assumptions about art and national stereotypes.

Our thanks go to all the twenty-eight artists contributing original visual essays to this book. They challenge us by stretching and bending reality and thereby keep pushing the boundaries of perception. At the same time we salute our visitors and readers, whose curiosity and interest keep the ball rolling.

We are grateful to all those who support the independence of the Swiss Institute and its activities: our members and trustees, as well as our public contributors and corporate sponsors in the United States, in Switzerland, and in other countries. Last but not least, we wish to acknowledge the great spirit and energy of our staff and the artistic director and EXTRA curator, Marc-Olivier Wahler.

Dieter von Graffenried and Fabienne P. Abrecht
Co-Chairs, SI Swiss Institute - Contemporary Art, New York

The inspiration for this book and the corresponding exhibition can be found in the question posed by its subtitle: *How many extra layers can we graft onto reality before it collapses?* Aiming to define a new way of grasping the concept of reality, both book and exhibition play with the idea that it is never *grasped*. Rather, we cease to see any limit to reality; it is continuous, complex, and dense: too fast to halt, pin down, and take a measurement. Instead of grasping it, we glide with it, riding through the layers and folds of the real. Art no longer attempts to develop new worlds, nor to take intrepid journeys to the ends of the real; it instead surfs along reality's surfaces. The question of the real and its limits flows through the exhibition and the text, which accompanies it (pp. 28 – 49). In this new realm of gliding over reality, art takes on diverse forms to reveal the extreme elasticity of the real. The art of EXTRA develops as an oscillation, shaking up our interpretative system. It is the pump, which dilates and contracts our reality.

Published for the occasion of the group exhibition EXTRA at the Swiss Institute, this book is the result of a collaboration with twenty-eight artists or groups of artists. Eleven of them are part of the EXTRA exhibition, and the seventeen others have built a close relationship with the SI, having participated in exhibitions here in past two years. For this book, each artist has specially crafted a visual essay of eight to twelve pages. These inserts are complemented by different texts: David Deutsch and Seth Lloyd, quantum physicists, deliver a passionate round of "Brain Tennis," in their exchange of correspondence discussing the concept of multiple universes. The ephemeral texts of Martin Tupper appear throughout the book, as nonsensical transmissions from another reality. The texts of art critic Bob Nickas and several of the artists (John Giorno, Jutta Koether, Olivier Mosset, Steven Parrino) serve to round out and complete this multilayered collaboration.

Marc-Olivier Wahler
Artistic Director, S I Swiss Institute - Contemporary Art, New York

MAKE YOUR OWN EXTRA →

INSTRUCTIONS FOR THE FOLLOWING PAGES

Cut out the floor plans of the S I exhibition space and art works
from the EXTRA show. Curate your own EXTRA!

Xerox or download the diagrams
and images from the next 4 pages.

(http://www.swissinstitute.net/Exhibitions/2003_Extra/do_it.html)

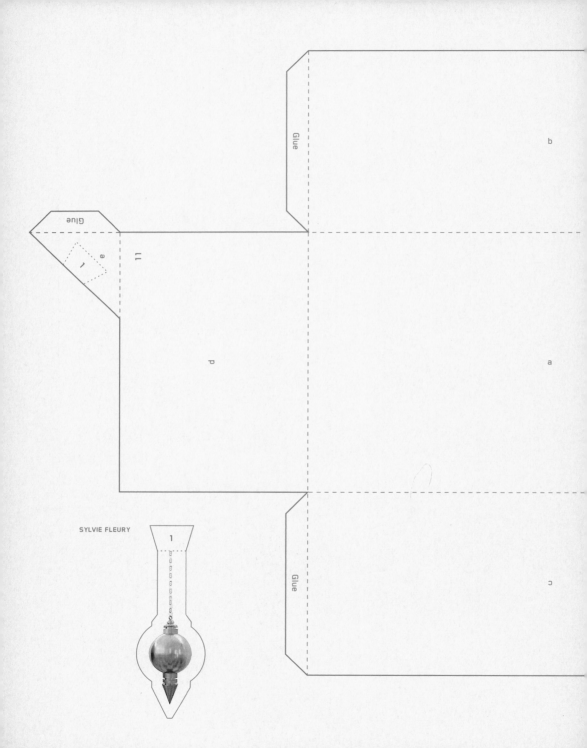

Glue

b

Glue

11 e 1

d

a

Glue

c

SYLVIE FLEURY

1

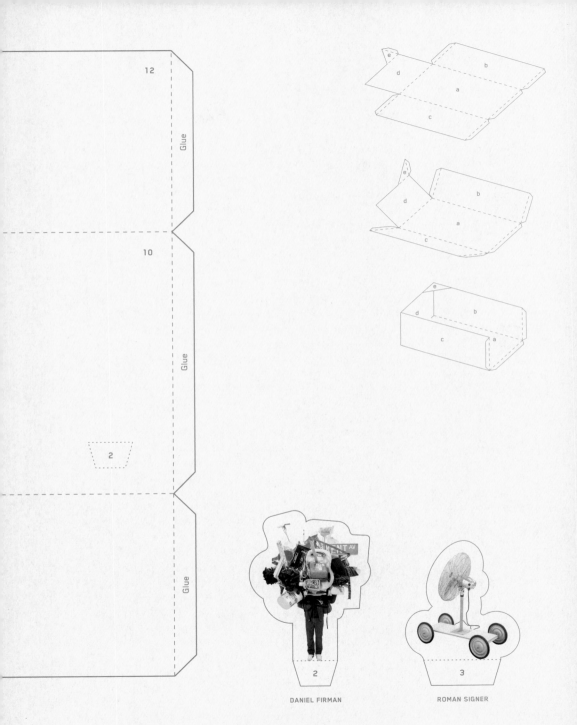

12

Glue

10

Glue

2

Glue

e

d

b

a

c

e

d

b

a

c

e

d

b

a

c

2

DANIEL FIRMAN

3

ROMAN SIGNER

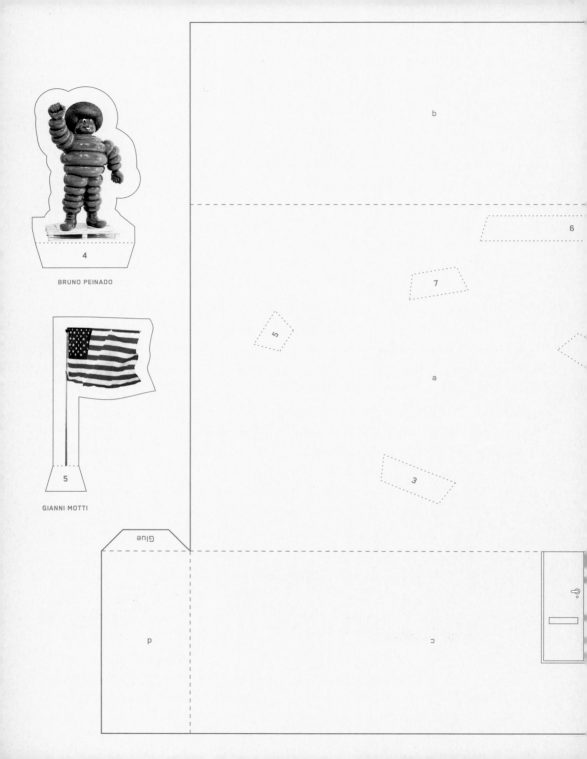

BRUNO PEINADO

GIANNI MOTTI

Glue

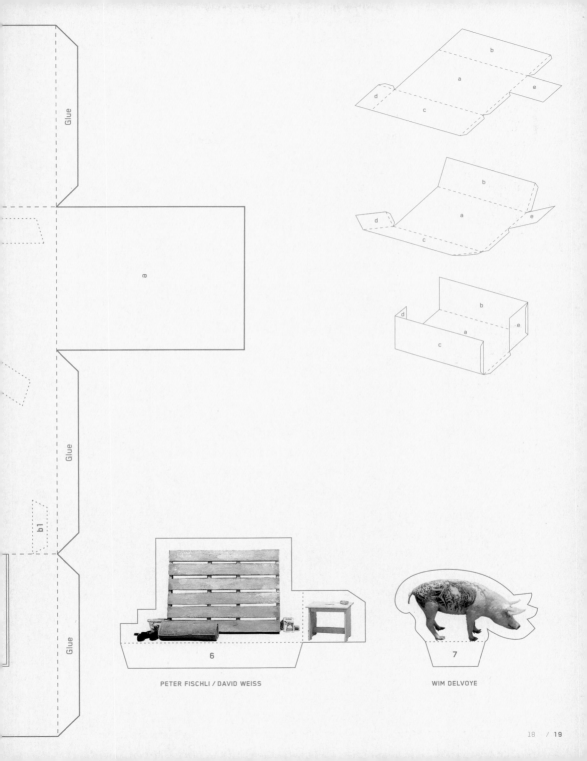

Glue

Glue

Glue

b1

a

b

a

c

d

e

b

a

c

d

e

b

a

c

d

e

6

PETER FISCHLI / DAVID WEISS

7

WIM DELVOYE

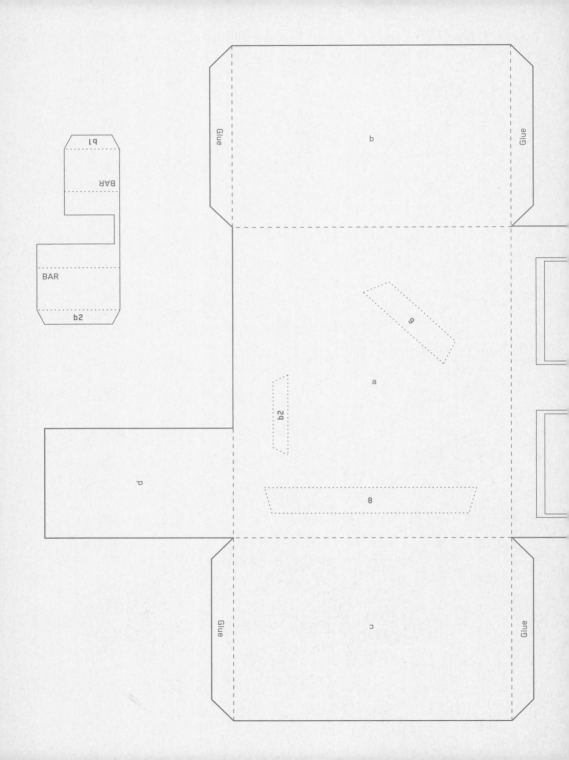

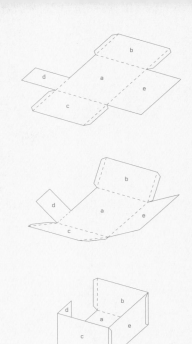

8

OLIVIER BLANCKART

9

STÉPHANE SAUTOUR

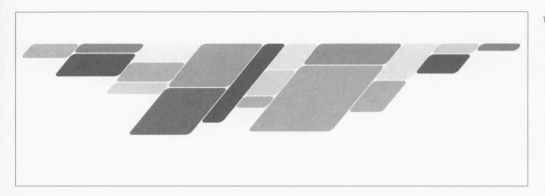

12

11

STÉPHANE DAFFLON

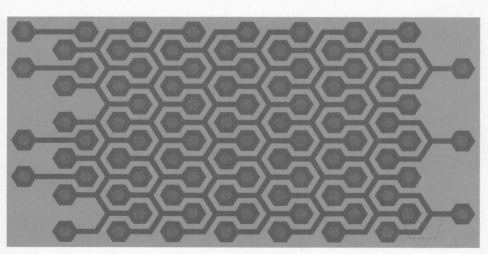

10

VIRGINIE BARRÉ

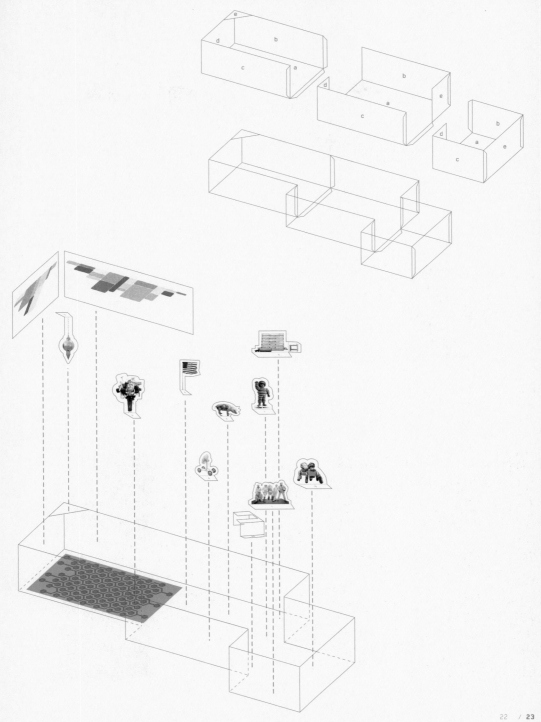

← EXTRA

HOW MANY EXTRA LAYERS CAN WE GRAFT ONTO REALITY
BEFORE IT COLLAPSES?

WITH: VIRGINIE BARRÉ, OLIVIER BLANCKART, STÉPHANE DAFFLON,
WIM DELVOYE, PETER FISCHLI / DAVID WEISS, SYLVIE FLEURY,
DANIEL FIRMAN, GIANNI MOTTI, BRUNO PEINADO, STÉPHANE SAUTOUR,
ROMAN SIGNER

CURATED BY MARC-OLIVIER WAHLER

A GROUP EXHIBITION AT
THE SWISS INSTITUTE – CONTEMPORARY ART, NEW YORK
MARCH 5 – APRIL 26, 2003

EXTRA

Never get out of the boat. Absolutely goddamn right.
Unless you were going all the way.

Captain Willard, Apocalypse Now

Summary of previous episodes

Mike Tyson not only serves as an extraordinary boxing phenomenon, he is also a key to understanding an entire field of contemporary art. When watching his fights on television, the power and speed with which Tyson throws his punches confront the viewer with issues of the furtive and the photogenic. One of my favorite tapes is *The Best Knockouts of Mike Tyson*. What always strikes me, as the unfortunate challenger falls each time, is Tyson's punch. His knockout is always invisible, a punch so swift it is delivered without any visual information: it is stealthy. Simultaneously, it is so brutal that it is photogenic. In slow motion we see Tyson initiate the attack and then, suddenly, his opponent drops like a dead man to the canvas – the transitionless knockout of Iron Mike. Neither the spectator nor (quite obviously!) the opponent has seen the punch in its entirety (its duration or its trajectory). If it is invisible, in what sense is it a part of our reality, and how can it also become spectacular? The fascination that Tyson holds for the common mortal is this paradoxical double manifestation: the contradiction between his furtive imperceptibility and his spectacular photogenic qualities. These two notions have become key concepts in recent years, used by a number of contemporary artists in understanding the codes of representation and the construction of new realities.

Episode 14
BOXING, APOCALYPSE, RAPE,
AND CONTEMPORARY ART

The notion of furtiveness or stealth, having its origins in the lexicon of military strategy, has slammed like a shock wave into the language of contemporary art. The furtive has nothing to do with camouflage. The aim of camouflage is to conceal; a camouflaged object takes on forms and colors that allow it to pass, not as invisible, but as unperceived. It is hidden; it is dressed-up. We are in the presence of the techniques of the primal hunt, or the strategies of a warrior from a century ago. Now a fashion statement (though certain armies still use this old method because it is cheap), in the eyes of warriors today, camouflage represents the methods of a coward. Camouflage is left to the lowest-ranking soldiers, playing the game of "hide and seek." In street fighting, for example, he who has to hide is pathetic, a wimp, a weakling, a pussy.

The furtive implies something totally different. Its main quality is to break all optical signals: it deflects, splits or absorbs… it doesn't hide, but rather evades being detected as visible. But the furtive object can, in a flash, become perfectly visible to the naked eye. The furtive (the lack of the visible) can transform itself into its exact opposite: the photogenic (excess of the visible). A *bombardier furtif* (stealth bomber), for example, evades radar detection: according to its instruments of measurement, it is invisible, absent. But the human eye has no trouble seeing it. At one moment it is visible, then it becomes not only vulnerable, but above all, hyper-spectacular, photogenic. Invisible and hyper-spectacular: such an object describes an absolutely stupefying paradox that has not escaped the attention of artists.

BEAST OF THE APOCALYPSE

Mike Tyson is an ideal example of this paradox. If he is the creature who is capable of beating his opponent by an invisible punch – which seems to come from nowhere, and which finishes its course right in the face of his challenger – then he embodies the model of a hyper-spectacular event. Seen on television, his punches rise up out of nothingness. It is in the invisible margins between frames, in the instants between the 24 frames per second that make up the film, the image of our reality. This paradox of the furtive resides completely in Tyson. His punches escape the vigilance of the cathode ray, leaving no visible trace: visually, they do not exist. But at the same time, what is left for us to see is hyper-spectacular, evidence of the excess of the visible: a superhero with his opponent on the ground. The impact of this striking image is multiplied by the personality of the boxer: a champion accused of rape, who has renounced any self-control, crushing anyone who gets in his way, whether it is the driver who does not give him the right of way; Miss Black America, who delays getting to her knees for him; the referee who dares stop his massacre; or, more recently, the bodyguard of his future opponent, who makes a gesture that seems suspicious. If he does not crush his opponent, Mike Tyson bites him savagely, in an act more similar to cannibalism than to a fighting technique.

Mike Tyson is the contemporary incarnation of the Beast of the Apocalypse: "Tyson may be everything those people say he is. The bad guy. The animal. The madman. But unlike those who call him names, he is not a hypocrite. He is exactly what everyone wants him to be (...) He went to prison for rape. He knocked his opponents to the ground. He has offered to break someone's arm (...) For the past 10 years, Tyson has been less a fighter than a horror film creature. He is a catastrophe waiting to happen, that messy wreck that you slow down to gawk at from the side of the road. That is what makes a Tyson fight must-see TV, even if you have to pay for it." [1]

THE RAPED RAPIST

Even if such behavior assures a boxer planetary glory and a colossal fortune, Mike Tyson knows, however, that it would be in his best interest to behave more delicately. It would have kept him out of prison, would have saved him from the vast condemnation of the media and kept him from being banned from boxing. Somewhere in him he would like to be known and recognized solely for his boxing abilities. But in the back of his head, there is always this voice that pushes him to ignore the sirens of political correctness and drives him to act in accord with his image as the diabolical exterminator. And so he fights. He fights as long as he can, until somehow he will fit into the standards of civilized society, where man respects woman and drivers wave amicably at each other on the road, where the athlete shakes hands with his valorous opponent – an ideal society, defined by a warm solidarity, a respect without discrimination, and a permanent smile. "Iron Mike" is ready for all necessary sacrifices to join this other world: he takes antidepressants; he married the charming Sarah Tyson, whom the department of education of Santa Fe called an excellent student of fine arts, an expert in pastels, oil painting, and gastronomy.[2] Mike even embraces Islam, an obligatory move for a black boxer who has spent more than six months in prison. He fights; and each time he seems to approach social acceptability (*Come on Mike, it's ok! We forgive you! Mike, smile at the journalists! Mike, say that you love this yogurt. Mike, sign here at the bottom right!*), a voice resounds that pushes him to sabotage these efforts (*No, Mike, don't let yourself be bewitched by these bland social niceties, refuse this predictable image of the "good black," who has succeeded in this white world. Mike, you are not Colin Powell, you are the terror of the streets, the ladies' nightmare, the bin Laden of boxing... ATTACK MIKE!!*).

Mike is stuck. Whether he opts to ascend toward the top of social correctness or plunge into the cauldron of the apocalypse, the outcome is equally fatal. Whatever his choice, half of his character will violate the other. He is in a constant state of individual forced-entry, *the raped rapist;* his soul breaks in two, and he continues to lash out against his adversaries, his wives, and all others who cross his path. From the furtive to the photogenic, Mike Tyson glides on the surface of reality, without being able to pinpoint what reality is, without being able to freeze it and take a measurement. He attempts to pierce through these slippery layers of the real, by slaughtering his entourage. But like the carnival game whack-a-mole, the real always reveals itself again and unexpectedly from another opening.

The older Mike gets, the farther he gets from the modernist model where we easily accept Iron Mike (and other artists or athletes) as an invincible knight, blessed by a power from another planet or as an extraterrestrial who has, against his will, taken on human form, but determined to show planet Earth that he is NOT human and will destroy every last one of us. His strength becomes weak against the effects of the real. In the end, his opponent winds up making his mark by sending him to prison or to the canvas. The whole of Mike's life alternates between these two states: the *superman*, the alien or hyper-spectacular superhero (who seemed real at the beginning, but has become inexorably transformed into history or even into a legend), and the *subhuman*, a figure exploited from all angles, a furtive shadow, looking for his soul. The story of Mike Tyson could be summarized in the title of a film: *Le Fabuleux destin de violeur violé*. [3] The rape analogy permits us to return to the concepts of the furtive and photogenic. If one of the particularities of an object endowed with both excess and absence of the visible is that it breaks its optical signature, then its ultimate mission is to invade and rape a territory, to penetrate a zone by any means, no matter how soft, deceptive, invisible, and furtive, no matter how exposed, violent, spectacular, and photogenic.

Many artists today articulate their ideas using models inspired by the paradoxes of the furtive and the photogenic. They develop strategies of infiltration, multiply networks, and bend the rules of the visible. They no longer stand on the same level as the romantic hero, looking down on the rest of the world, like so many John Waynes on white horses. They glide on the surface of the landscape. Knowing that reality is no longer a territory to conquer and penetrate, but more of a climate-controlled supermarket full of information – a place of transit where movement is imperative – they adjust their cruising speeds to match that of their next-door neighbor. They infiltrate into the realm of the commuting masses, anesthetized by the banality of their quotidian gestures. They adopt a principle of constant mobility, and seem to confirm this "indifference that from now on affects the real." [4] And when they act like they are coming to a halt, reality seems to be turned upside down. One simple detail from what is normally invisible takes on a spectacular dimension. It becomes photogenic. New paradigms emerge... without warning, artists have slipped into our interpretative systems.

At once demonic and media-conscious, they operate under the eyes of everyone, but in the margin, in this wrinkle which folds into itself to the infinite, in constant transit, which renders their actions at once invisible and hyper-spectacular, anonymous and scandalous.

Episode 15
GLIDING

When he is invited by art centers or galleries to "create an event" for the night of an opening, Gianni Motti is very careful to avoid making a personal performance piece. He disappears and leaves his space to actors from the real world. In Geneva, on September 27, 1997, Motti diverted the route of a bus full of Japanese tourists. After the tour guide had fallen under his charms, he convinced her that an opening reception at the Centre de Gravure would be much more interesting than a visit to the United Nations. At 6 P.M., fifty Japanese tourists arrived smack in the middle of the opening. Hilarious: they began taking pictures in front of works by Trockel together with the Geneva natives, and, with copious amounts of free white wine, listened attentively to the explanation of their guide, then disappeared in their bus. The art center had wanted Gianni Motti to enliven the opening; what occurred transformed it into a tourist attraction. In Paris, on March 20, 1998, devotees of the Raëlian sect made an appearance during an opening at the gallery Jousse/Seguin. As they are accustomed, the Raëlians looked right into the eyes of their spectators and evoked the glory of their god: an alien who came to Earth and cloned himself to make the human race. The "chance encounters" between Gianni Motti and a group of tourists or the descendants of aliens can seem at first like the consequence of coincidence. Looked at more closely, such encounters strikingly enlighten the approach of this artist.

Gianni Motti strolls along as a tourist. Like many artists today, he does not go on grand expeditions, like a tormented Fitzcarraldo, ready to fight with anyone who blocks his path. He glides on the interior of the spectacle. When asked (ten years ago), which television personality had the most impact on the public, Umberto Eco put Columbo at the top of the list. [5] If we polled artists today, Columbo would without a doubt also win the vote, even though he is certainly not as talented as Superman: he cannot fly faster than a speeding bullet and doesn't possess the powers of super-hearing or X-ray vision. Like Gianni Motti and his peers, Columbo strolls along, arousing his curiosity from the course of a conversation, buys his clothes at Walmart, and enjoys a few drinks, just like anyone. "The truth will be revealed anyway," which Columbo often says, could be Gianni's motto as well. His investigative tactics involve no heroics: they always wind up in a confession, the guilty party collapsing under the weight of Columbo's insinuations. Like Columbo, or any tourist, artists today trust in their intuition as much as in the coincidence of circumstance. Like new pirates, they no longer fight head on, with a menacing voice and weapons loaded. They develop strategies of infiltration, elaborate parallel networks, and distort the rules of the visible.

An encounter between Gianni Motti and the descendants of aliens is also illuminating. The image of the hysterical little green man who waves his laser gun around and pulverizes everything that gets in his way is outdated. For a while now, the representation of aliens has grown to resemble that of human beings. Either man is the clone of aliens or the extraterrestrial takes on the appearance of human beings. The latter is fascinating: it sheds an interesting light on contemporary art. It is only by the tiniest evidence that the alien's disguise is betrayed (a pinky finger that is too stiff, for example). Once identified, he recovers his alien status. He then immediately disappears from our view. But has he really left our reality? Can he really have pierced through the exterior of the real?

MULTIVERSE, VIDEO GAMES, AND QUANTUM PHYSICS

Extraterrestrials perform a precise function, aside from the diversion they provide on television on a rainy Sunday afternoon. They help us to develop a notion of reality that is more complex than our common sense has ever strived to build. If our world seems more real to us than another, it is not from experience (because each world seems uniquely real to its inhabitants), but from a philosophical conception that has been historically imposed on our common sense. [6]

Another item that interferes with the construction of the notion of a more expansive reality: video games. Since their recent ascent, each player has grown accustomed to having numerous lives at his disposal. Moreover, he does not gain a better life by adhering to a rigorous code of ethics; it is only by the agility with which he maneuvers through the world he chooses to play in.

Thanks to astronomy, we have retained the possibility of imagining an expansive and complex reality. The first exoplanet [7] was observed less than a decade ago and today we discover more practically each day. Such findings allow a belief in the possibility that there is life outside of our solar system. Given the number of exoplanets that have been actually observed, we should admit that, statistically, the hypothesis that life exists elsewhere in the universe is more possible than the idea that we are the unique life form.

But perhaps it is quantum physics, which brings new clarity to our notion of reality. David Deutsch, professor of Quantum Physics at the Centre for Quantum Computation at Oxford, has demonstrated with his research that while there could be many universes, there is only one overarching reality. In a correspondence, reproduced in this catalogue, Deutsch explains that reality should not be judged in relation to a universe, but rather in relation to a "multiverse": "Reality consists of a multiverse, an enormous entity which, *on a gross scale,* has a structure that resembles many copies of the universe of classical physics, but which is, on a sufficiently fine scale, a single, unified system." [8] In an interview with *Philosophy Now*, Deutsch further explains his ideas about parallel universes. Here is a lengthy quotation from this interview, in which he explains in more detail his thinking on parallel universes:

"Let's start with the microscopic world, because it is only at the microscopic level that we have direct evidence of parallel universes. The first stage in the argument is to note that the behavior of particles in the single slit experiment reveals there are processes going on that we do not see but which we can detect because of their interference effects on things that we do see. The second step is to note that the complexity of this unseen part of the microscopic world is much greater than that which we do see. And the strongest illustration of that is in quantum computation where we can tell that a moderate-sized quantum computer could perform computations of enormous complexity, greater complexity than the entire visible universe with all the atoms that we see, all taking place within a quantum computer consisting of just a few hundred atoms. So there is a lot more in reality than what we can see. What we can see is a tiny part of reality and the rest of it most of the time does not affect us. But in these special experiments some parts of it do affect us, and even those parts are far more complicated than the whole of what we see. The only remaining intermediate step is to see that quantum mechanics, as we already have it, describes these other parts of reality, the parts that we don't see, just as much as the parts we do see. It also describes the interaction of the two, and when we analyze the structure of the unseen part we see that to a very good approximation, it consists of many copies of the part that we can see. It is not that there is a monolithic 'other universe' which is very complicated and has different rules or whatever. The unseen part behaves very like the seen part, except that there are many copies.

"It is rather like the discovery of other planets or other galaxies. Having previously known only the Milky Way, we did not just find that there are vast numbers of stars out there, far more than in the Milky Way. There are more galaxies out there than there are stars in the Milky Way. We also found that most of the stars outside the Milky Way are actually arranged in other little Milky Ways themselves. And that is exactly what happens with parallel universes. It is of course only an analogy but quite a good one; just like the stars and galaxies, the unseen parts of reality are arranged in groups that resemble the seen part. Within one of these groups, which we call a parallel universe, the particles all can interact with each other, even though they barely interact with particles in other universes. They interact in much the same way as the ones in our seen universe interact with each other. That is the justification for calling them universes. The justification for calling them parallel is that they hardly interact with each other, like parallel lines that do not cross. That is an approximation, because interference phenomena do make them interact slightly. So, that is the sequence of arguments that leads from the parallelism, which by the way is much less controversial at the microscopic level than the macroscopic level, right up to parallel universes. Philosophically, I would like to add to that that it simply does not make sense to say that there are parallel copies of all particles that participate in microscopic interactions, but that there are not parallel copies of macroscopic ones. It is like saying that someone is going to double the number of pennies in a bank account without doubling the number of Pounds."[9]

According to Deutsch, what we see only represents one tiny part of reality. Reality does not end with what we see or perceive, and the "rest," this "invisible," constitutes an undefined territory where an infinite number of worlds are organized (according to the experience of quantum physicists) in the same way that our visible world is. These are, in a sense, copies of our visible world, and they explain the seemingly absurd assertion that there is a copy of each of us in every universe, and that the totality of copies add up to one reality.

It is interesting to see the manner in which the notion of reality and of the invisible have evolved in art and the manner in which now art seems to be approaching the current pre-occupations of physicists. "To see the invisible" – the desire of many artists in the first half of the twentieth century – aimed at the exploration of a realm beyond the visible world. This territory was considered uncharted, a terra incognita that artists ventured into as explorers of the unconscious. In art as elsewhere, the hero left to conquer new lands and was expected to return a redeemer: thanks to the artist, reality gained new dimensions; it could be stretched and still survive. Extraterrestrials endowed with unstoppable weapons take over planet Earth, Superman overcame gravity to save planet Earth, and the artist used transcendental inspiration to uncover the many layers buried in planet Earth. Gliding over reality, over laws, physical and psychic constraints, all three could assign "mere mortals," a precise place embedded in reality. "To see the invisible": it was (in the best case) to unveil virgin territories, new regions, and platforms to occupy. But it indicated, above all, a "precise point," defined by what escaped our notion of reality, by what seemed beyond our common perception.

THE REAL: HOW MANY LAYERS?

Something totally different illuminates the art of today, which, not surprisingly, follows the same evolution as that of the hero, the extraterrestrials, and quantum physics. Remember Stalin's famous question, "The Pope: How many divisions has he got?" In the same way, today we could ask ourselves, "The real: How many layers has it got?" This question leads us to others: "*Up to what point can we stretch reality until it tears? How many layers can we graft onto reality before it collapses?*" Today, such questions seem just as absurd as the one posed by Stalin. Actually, the later the century advanced, the more reality mani-fested its complexity. The more we multiplied our efforts to analyze reality, the more reality revealed an incredible elasticity and so infinitely expandable and flexible. "There is no fixed point in the universe," confirmed Einstein. In the face of this terrifying assessment, it was necessary to get organized. The difficult mission of defining the precise boundaries where man could find his place (once the responsibility of superheroes of all kinds) has radically changed in the past few decades. Our current heroes get colds, have dandruff, watch their weight, have prostate problems, are sent to prison, and/or die of cancer. Pretty much like everyone else. There are no longer romantic utopias to perpetuate such a Mission Impossible. Usually, they are recruited into the sports world (because they run the longest or race the fastest), alternative sports (to travel around the world in a balloon or cross the arctic), or the world of cinema (to play Jesus or his reincarnations, specialists in redemption of all kinds, such as Napoleon, Gandhi, JFK, or Jim Morrison). But they can't keep up the illusion for long. Caught in the act of sniffing coke, committing tax fraud, scratching their crotch, or reading an IKEA catalogue, they are betrayed, either too soon or too late, by their humanity.

Let's face it: it becomes more and more difficult to live by proxy. We are certainly not lacking in candidates for deification, but none of them hold their power for more than a season. Confronted by this deficiency, the limits of reality become effaced, as inexorably as the desert's sprawling expanse. This is where contemporary philosophers find their greatest anguish: the present slides on the surface of time, making it impossible to grasp a reality marked by clearly delimited temporal reference points. Immersed in a global time-frame, we are witness to a compression of the past, present, and future, and we are transported into the immediate, into instantaneousness. Dominated by the notion of "real time," the present can only pass by,[10] in a movement of continuous transit, of perpetual gliding. Certain philosophers, such as Paul Virilio, are disturbed by such a situation, distinguished by the rupture in the markings of traditional time, where man can no longer (and no longer wants to) slow down this constant transfer, where he must lose all hope of regaining the common signs that define his condition of *being in the world*. How can we live in a universe devoid of limits, when the very search for these limits is necessary to maintain our equilibrium? Such a paradox is at the heart of the reflections shared by humanists of all varieties.

Generally considered as an obstacle to overcome, a problem to eradicate, *gliding* through the world constitutes a fantastic challenge for art. Rather than shunning this, contemporary art joins with it by adopting this very dynamic. The old notion of building new platforms has been left to the art of the past. No longer believing in the virtue of in-between spaces that had infiltrated the art of the 1990s, today's artists engage in an activity that can seem difficult or even dangerous. "A losing battle," their parents lament, shaking their heads. We retort, citing Ben's famous formula, "Art is a dirty job, but someone's gotta do it." Artists take to the extreme this propensity of letting themselves go, not resisting the expansive sprawl of the desert, to let themselves be caught up in the breaking waves that efface all tracks, all limits. Not that they have decided to turn off the television, to stop smoking, and to concentrate on the moral values of our society. No? they watch reality TV while drinking beer, sleep late, and read the tabloids. But rather than being defeated by this state and revolting every new year with a resolution that "this year I'll be better," they dive straight into it, gliding, like parasites, adopting their host's method of functioning. Following this model, the work of Peter Fischli / David Weiss is an exemplary case.

To be continued in the next episode.

Episode 16
WAITING FOR SUNDAY

In 1978, Peter Fischli / David Weiss set out to visit a big furniture store in the suburbs. They wandered endlessly before stopping – astonished – before a Moroccan pouffe. A year later, they began an artistic collaboration which we now judge – twenty-five years later – to be an extraordinarily rich and inventive one.

Analyzing a work of Peter Fischli / David Weiss can arouse feelings of vertigo, not unlike the sequences and dynamic movements in their famous 1987 film, *Der Lauf der Dinge* (The Way Things Go): each thing is the cause of the one that comes after it; every object is included in a chain reaction, and this frantic succession seems to know no end, not focused on any particular concept, barely identifiable.

What is the causal link between a slice of mortadella, a sewer pipe, a snowman, a cauliflower, a concrete landscape, a gherkin balanced on a carrot, some bread, a train, an airport tarmac, multicolored flowers, a polyurethane bucket and the pyramids?

By 1984, Peter Fischli / David Weiss had established a prioritized list of questions that needed answering: *Is everything just a question of time? Should I change the bedsheets? Is there life in outer space? Do they love me? How far can one go? Can we make everything up? Do you want another drink?*[11]

Where are the answers? Peter Fischli smiles and speaks of a "schizophrenia of feelings." We might add: *gliding over feelings.* Because, who really looks at their images, for example, the purposely banal photographs called *Bilder, Ansichten* (Pictures, Views, 1991)? They show what everyone knows, that which is inscribed in our collective visual memory. To see, and to show, what common sense expects: a reassuring illustration, a beautiful image, is something that we immediately decipher and whose codes are unanimously shared.[12] Archetypal images. The pyramids, airports, sunsets on the beach, the Eiffel Tower, a newborn kitten, red apples drenched in sun, the Matterhorn, the Grand Canyon. The pictures we have seen a thousand times on every postcard, and of which John Waters, the prince of bad taste, has asked, "Who was the first to talk about airports?"[13] before confessing that he saw a new type of beauty in these clichés, a new kind of work of art, about which there is really nothing left to say. To see the Matterhorn one more time, or a sunset on the beach is not disagreeable. In any case, we do not really look at these images that we always have before our eyes. We glide over them to think of other things: of last year's vacation, in that amazing chalet; of that television series we watch on Sunday afternoon.

FILLING TIME. IN PRAISE OF SLOWNESS AND THE AESTHETIC OF GLIDING

These photographs are not readymade. Peter Fischli / David Weiss were not content to dip into a vast image bank to find the pictures that seemed, to their eyes, most significant. The voyage, wandering, waiting for the perfect moment, the desire to succeed in creating clichés that would leave nothing to desire of the most beautiful postcards, were all important elements. The desire to feel the power and the acquired aura of the ready-made can be seen in the works of a totally different nature, as in for example, *Der Tisch* (The Table, 1992). On an immense wooden table, a mess of eclectic objects, from cleaning fluid to dog food to paint cans, bricks, chocolate, stools, paintbrushes, empty containers, a telephone, a can of Coke, etc. It could be an ensemble of objects found in the artists' studio, except for the fact that the exhibited elements on the table were all meticulously fabricated in polyurethane, a material that these artists have worked with since the beginning of their career. Other works have been made in rubber, like the Moroccan pouffe, made in 1987. A readymade isn't made; it appears suddenly, transfigured from one state to another. In a passionate essay Boris Groys revealed that the work of art reached the speed of light in the last century, when its production became as fast as thought and it no longer relied on anything more than making a decision.[14] Peter Fischli / David Weiss, however, propose a vast enterprise of deceleration. The works that they elaborate are not distinguishable from our everyday objects. We wait to find the trace of manufacturing, evidence of our machine age. We find, instead, handmade objects, painstakingly executed by artisans. It is not about exalting the virtues of the craftsman, for Peter Fischli / David Weiss. The slowness is related to time, and for them, "hard work is time wasted wisely." Slowness can also be a kind of wandering, that of the *flânerie*. It is, then linked to the existential question: How can I fill time usefully? What can I do Sunday afternoon? What will I see if I go out wandering? In general, nothing. We walk in settings that will nourish our waking dreams.

It is this "nothing in particular" that Peter Fischli/David Weiss set out to depict with a work presenting over eighty hours of video on twelve monitors (XLVI Venice Biennial, 1995). The artists had filmed the route between their house and their studio, an excursion in the Alps, an indoor motorcross course, cheese making. In Zurich, they still wander, watching people washing their cars, buying sausages at a stand. No commentary is given. No attempt is made to differentiate from the neutral television aesthetic. It seems like sequences from "No Comment" from Euronews. But nothing happens. No one is shot in the crowd. The artists simply film what interests them at the moment. When we are filling time, we are on the lookout for the smallest event. We establish a hierarchy of interesting things. We choose to follow a scene, even the most insignificant, over another. We wait until "something happens" and in life, as in the videos of Peter Fischli/David Weiss, it is rare that something happens. So we wait. And this waiting for something essential often constitutes the essence what we are waiting for. We wait for Sunday with impatience. On Sunday, however, as we know, we find ourselves bored, and it is finally this waiting itself which is revealed as the most passionate moment.

Peter Fischli/David Weiss have a taste for *flânerie*. During one year they took to photographing flowers, onions and vegetable gardens, using a beginner's technique: the double exposure. The result is perplexing. "How beautiful!" we exclaim spontaneously, while at the same time we become critical, worried that we should not be so impressionable. These double exposures of natural beauty inspire mixed emotions, recalling the "schizophrenia of feelings" referred to earlier. In an installation first shown in 1999, Peter Fischli/David Weiss projected these images onto gallery walls.[15] Thanks to the technique of crossfading, each slide – the result of a double exposure – overlapped with the next, helped by the uninterrupted rotation of the carousel. This quadruple exposure was breathtaking. Faced with the total absence of fixed points, the eye could only glide over the images. A staggered view, intoxicated by the illusion of continuous movement to which cinema has made us accustomed. Vision was no longer experimenting with observation, but with a journey. But, as opposed to cinema, we are part of a boundless journey, without beginning or end, a journey that endlessly *passes through*. And like their images, marching through their double-exposure, the artists are endlessly *passing through*.

Contrary to the protagonists of Land Art – who left their studios to go *on the road,* to travel the breadth of the gigantic American expanse, in search of sites to besiege – artists of today do not besiege anything at all. They do not go out on expeditions; they wander. They no longer situate themselves out in the landscape; they glide on the inside of it. Wandering possesses one important virtue, which makes it both useful and life-saving: it fills time. And rather than being subjected to the incessant movement of transit that makes up our "real time," wandering allows artists to adapt their speeds to the instantaneousness of our present and develop a true *aesthetic of gliding*.

Translated from the French by Gabrielle Giattino.

FEATURING, IN ORDER OF APPEARANCE

CAPTAIN WILLARD – MIKE TYSON – THE OPPONENT – THE AUDIENCE – THE ARTISTS – THE DRIVER
MISS BLACK AMERICA – THE REFEREE – THE BODYGUARD – THE ATHLETE – SARAH TYSON
COLIN POWELL – BIN LADEN – THE EXTRATERRESTRIAL – JOHN WAYNE – THE NEXT-DOOR NEIGHBOR
GIANNI MOTTI – ROSEMARIE TROCKEL – THE JAPANESE AND THEIR TOUR GUIDE – THE RAËLIANS
FITZCARRALDO – UMBERTO ECO – COLUMBO – SUPERMAN – DAVID DEUTSCH – STALIN – THE POPE
EINSTEIN – JESUS – NAPOLEON – GANDHI – JFK – JIM MORRISON – PAUL VIRILIO – BEN
PETER FISCHLI / DAVID WEISS – JOHN WATERS – BORIS GROYS

1   Wallace Matthews, "The Freak Show Much Go On; Money's the Root of
    Tyson's Evil Acts," *New York Post*, January 23, 2002.

2   "She is an avid golfer, helps steer FOCA and creates gourmet meals.
    She is married to Mike Tyson and has both ears. Sarah has been a docent
    at SITE Santa Fe for five years."
    http://www.sitesantafe.org/general/contacts.html

3   In English: *The Fabulous Destiny of the Raped Rapist*. The French makes
    reference to the title of the film *Amélie*, as it was in France: "Le Fabuleux
    destin d'Amélie Poulin."

4   Gilles Lipovetsky, *L'ère du vide* (Paris : Gallimard, 1983), p. 107.

5   Umberto Eco, "Conclusion 1993," in *De Superman au surhomme*,
    (Paris: Grasset, 1993), p. 210.

6   See David Deutsch and Seth Lloyd, "Are Parallel Universes Equally Real?
    Brain Tennis," *HotWired*,
    http://www.hotwired.lycos.com/synapse/braintennis/97/41/index0a.html
    (reprinted in this catalogue).

7   A planet outside of our solar system.

8   David Deutsch and Seth Lloyd, "Are Parallel Universes Equally Real?
    Brain Tennis," p. 7.

9   Interview with Filiz Peach, *Philosophy Now*, 30, December 2000.

10 "Ce monde tel que nous le voyons est en train de passer" *The world as
    we see it, is engaged in passing us*. Paul de Tarse, cited by Paul Virilio,
    Esthétique de la disparition (Paris: Galilée, 1989), p. 9.

11 *Fragentopf*. The questions were inscribed into the bottom of
    a polyurethane vase.

12 It is impossible to know if they took these photos as souvenirs from a trip,
    or if they took the trip to take these photos. Christophe Donimo, "Petit
    encyclopédie portative," in *Peter Fischli / David Weiss* (Paris: Musée
    national d'art moderne, éd. Centre Georges Pompidou, 1992).

13 John Waters, "Airports," *Vogue* (New York), 1990.

14 Boris Groys, "The Speed of Art," in *Peter Fischli / David Weiss*
    (Venice and Bern: XLVI Bienniale di Venezia, éd. OFC, Berne, 1985).

15 Musée d'art moderne de la Ville de Paris.

Are Parallel Universes Equally Real?

Our "twins" in parallel universes are just as real as we are, says David Deutsch. The notion that our world is somehow more real is derived not from experience (since each "world" seems equally real to its inhabitants), nor from quantum mechanics (in an absolute sense there are no splits at all, and there is no moment when your unseen counterparts can no longer affect you – it just gets very expensive to measure the effects), but ultimately from the pernicious influence of a sterile branch of philosophy.

Seth Lloyd endorses the description given by quantum mechanics of a universe that is constantly branching into different "worlds," but insists that he and the world he inhabits are real in a way that his "twins" in parallel worlds are not. When the universe splits into decohering branches ("quantum decoherence"), the split is irrevocable, and, for all intents and purposes, the other branches and their corresponding worlds don't exist: "The branch of the universe in which pigs fly exists only when pigs actually fly."

Dear David,

I am writing to relate to you a strange thing that happened to me a few weeks ago
in the MIT bookstore. I was standing in front of a bookshelf, trying to decide whether
to buy your new book or Roger Penrose's. Now as you know, neurons are notoriously
sensitive cells, capable of amplifying very small effects. As a result of a tiny quantum-
mechanical fluctuation, a few extra transmitter chemicals jumped across one of my
synapses and bound to the receptors on a neuron. This extra stimulation pushed the
neuron over its threshold and caused it to fire, triggering a burst of neural activity and
causing me, on impulse, to buy your book, *The Fabric of Reality*. Upon reading this book,
I discovered that you espouse the so-called "many worlds" interpretation of quantum
mechanics, in which every quantum fluctuation causes the world to split into different
parts, each one of which is equally real. You seem to be implying that in another equally
real world there is another me, equally real, who is currently reading Penrose's book.
How dare you imply this! I really bought your book, I really like it, and I really prefer
to be reading it rather than Penrose's book. Who are you to say that imposter in the
other world is just as real as me? I await your response.

Yours sincerely,
Seth Lloyd

Dear Seth,

I'm glad you enjoyed *The Fabric of Reality,* but are you sure that you chose it randomly? Most readers, I'm sure, buy it as a result of rational thought, in which case most of their counterparts in parallel universes buy it too. But to the extent that your decision did depend on random events, there are indeed other, equally real, versions of you in other universes, who chose differently and are now enduring the consequences.

Why do I believe this? Mainly because I believe quantum mechanics. Just write down the equation describing the motion of those fateful transmitter molecules, and their effect on you and on the environment. Notice that their "randomness" consists in their doing two things at once: crossing that synapse and not crossing it; and that the effect on you was likewise that you did two things at once: buy my book and buy Penrose's. Such effects spread out, making everything do many things at once, which is what we mean by saying that there are "parallel universes."

Furthermore, the universes affect each other. Though the effects are minute, they are detectable in carefully designed experiments. There are projects under way – close to your heart, I know, as well as mine – to harness these effects to perform useful computations. When a quantum computer solves a problem by dividing it into more sub-problems than there are atoms in the universe, and then solving each sub-problem, it will prove to us that those sub-problems were solved *somewhere* – but not in our universe, for there isn't enough room here. What more do you need to persuade you that other universes exist?

Yours sincerely,
David

Dear David,

Thank you for your response: I feel sorry for the other me in the parallel universe who accidentally bought Penrose's book and is debating him instead. But since I'm really debating you and not Penrose, I don't understand why you refer to my shadowy twin in the parallel universe as equally real. Call me old-fashioned, but I like to refer to things in *this* universe as real: I really had toast, not cereal, for breakfast; I really drank tea, not coffee; and I really am writing this letter to David, not Roger. The toast, the tea, and this letter are real in a way that my Penrose-reading twin is not: The toast can satisfy my hunger, the tea my thirst, and our correspondence my curiosity, but nothing that my parallel twin can do can make any difference to me, to you, or to anyone in this universe that we really do inhabit.

The reason that my twin can make no difference lies in the physical phenomenon of decoherence. As you know, decoherence is a process that robs quantum states of their ability to interfere with one another. The hotter and more intrusive the environment of a quantum system, the more rapidly decoherence takes place. I'm a mammal, you're a mammal. The mammalian brain is a hot, wet place. Within a tiny fraction of a second after the quantum fluctuation had taken place that set in motion the chain of events that caused me to buy your book rather than Penrose's, the universe in which the neuron fired and my hand reached to D had separated irrevocably from the universe in which the neuron didn't fire and my hand reached to P. (The tendency of the brain to decohere its contents is the reason Penrose's claims for the importance of quantum coherence for consciousness should be regarded with skepticism.) Once decoherence has taken place, my twin can no longer interfere with me, and has ceased to be real in the way that you, who can argue with me, are.

Quantum computers, in contrast to our brains, operate coherently. I am comfortable with the notion of a quantum system such as a photon being many places at once – my eye wouldn't function unless each photon passed through all points in the lens simultaneously. Why then can't a quantum computer effectively perform many computations simultaneously without the universe splitting into many parts?

Yours sincerely,
Seth

Dear Seth,

So you admit that photons, atoms, and quantum computations have invisible, differently behaving counterparts, but you still cling to the belief that *you* exist in only one copy. I don't think this makes sense, because you are made of atoms, and if they have invisible counterparts, so must you.

Look inside a quantum computer during a computation. The particular set of values you see in its registers corresponds to one particular computation – but you agree that, in fact, it was performing vast numbers of other computations at the same time, computations of which you detected no trace. Now, in the example you gave, quantum mechanics describes *you* as performing two different computations (viz., reading two different books). Yet you maintain that when you check your own memory and remember reading *The Fabric of Reality,* then that is the only reading that has been going on. Your excuse for treating these two cases differently, when their quantum-mechanical descriptions are perfectly analogous, is that the quantum computer gives you an output which depends logically on vast numbers of invisible computations, so you must accept that they really happened. By contrast, the other computations that quantum mechanics says that *you* performed (such as reading Penrose's book) can never affect you because of decoherence, so you prefer to believe that they never happened. But decoherence is just a matter of degree. There is never a moment after which an object's invisible counterparts *cannot* affect it any longer. It just gets too expensive to set up the apparatus that would demonstrate their existence. To claim that if something is too expensive to measure, it doesn't exist, is surely just a perverse form of solipsism.

Shoot a photon out into an empty region of the night sky. Unlike decoherence, this is a truly irrevocable act: If you change your mind, the laws of physics say you'll never retrieve the photon. Yet you wouldn't deny that it still exists, would you? The proper criterion for whether something exists is not whether it can still affect us, but whether *it figures in our best explanation* of what affects us. To deny the existence of that photon, or of those invisible computations, or invisible universes, is to renounce explanation of what we do see.

Yours sincerely,
David

Dear David,

You champion the existence of multiple me's and assert their equal claim to reality;
I insist on my prior claim, since I am really debating you while the other me's are not.
Rather than imitating my daughter and repeating "me me me" until you give up, let me
try to first find where we agree and then where we differ. I think that we agree that
that quantum description of the universe (the "wave function") is constantly branching
into different "worlds," in one of which we are debating now, in another of which I am
debating Penrose, and in others (I hope the plurality) of which we are amicably sipping
margaritas on the beach. Each one of these "worlds" seems equally real to its inhabitants, even if these multiple realities are mutually exclusive. In addition, quantum
mechanics picks out no one of these "worlds" or branches as special.

So far, so good. Now, as I understand your position, you assign all of these "worlds"
an equal measure of reality and claim they all exist. Here we differ. Arguing with
philosophers has made me wary of putting too great a burden of meaning on the words
"exist" and "real." But the conventional use of those words refers to objects and events
in our particular branch of the universe. The cup of tea that I am drinking exists; we
are really debating. In contrast, the other branches or "worlds" are exactly the parts
of the wave function in which the cup of tea does not exist and we are not really debating. These other "worlds" do not exist in the way that this one does. For better or
worse, I suspect that most people will believe that the branch of the universe in which
pigs fly exists only when pigs actually fly.

We differ on more than semantics, however. From your clear and elegant discussion of
quantum computation, I can tell that we differ also as to the point at which the universe
branches into different "worlds." You argue that one must accept the existence of the
other branches because these branches could interfere with our branch in the future.
For decoherence, however, the issue is not whether the branches *could* interfere with
each other, but rather whether they actually *do* interfere with each other at some time
in the future. Decoherent branches, by definition, do not interfere with each other:
As a result, when the universe splits into two decohering branches, the split is irrevocable, and for all intents and purposes the other branches and their corresponding
"worlds" do not exist.

In a quantum computation, as you point out, the branches actually do interfere with each other, allowing the computation of quantities, such as factors of large numbers, that are properties of all the branches taken together but not of any branch in particular. (This performance of the computation in many branches is at bottom no stranger than the single photon that, at your suggestion, I shot into the air last night occupying many points of space at once.) But the very fact that the quantum computer gives us an answer that depends on all the branches at once means that the universe has not really split: Those branches were part of our world, not of other worlds! The universe splits if and only if its branches decohere.

Thanks for a great debate, better than the one I had with Borges on the same subject. I met him at a garden party in Cambridge in the last year of his life, and asked whether he had quantum mechanics in mind when he wrote his wonderful evocation of a branching universe, "The Garden of Forking Paths." His answer: "No."

Yours,
Seth

Dear Seth,

Our disagreement is certainly about more than just semantics; however, your latest reply suggests that our positions may be closer than your forthright opening remarks might have indicated.

Our key area of agreement is, as you say, that what quantum mechanics *describes* is not a single universe but something that "is constantly branching into different 'worlds,' in one of which we are debating now, in another of which I am debating Penrose."

You also say: "The very fact that the quantum computer gives us an answer that depends on all the branches at once means that the universe has not really split: Those branches were part of our world, not of other worlds! The universe splits if and only if its branches decohere." I entirely agree! Reality consists of a multiverse, an enormous entity which, *on a gross scale,* has a structure that resembles many copies of the universe of classical physics, but which is, on a sufficiently fine scale, a single, unified system. In an absolute sense, there are never any splits at all.

Our key point of disagreement is that, despite the fact that "quantum mechanics picks out no one of these 'worlds' or branches as special," you still want to believe that "these other 'worlds' do not exist in the way that this one does."

If you are right, it surely follows that the thing that singles out our own branch as more real than all the others is nowhere to be found in quantum mechanics. Nor is it, of course, anywhere to be found in our experience, since, as you say, "each one of these 'worlds' seems equally real to its inhabitants." So where is it to be found?

It is found in (or rather, demanded by) philosophy – and in particular, I believe, by the sterile philosophy of positivism and related doctrines that have been impeding scientific progress for the last seventy-odd years. You say: "Arguing with philosophers has made me wary of putting too great a burden of meaning on the words 'exist' and 'real.'" There may lie your problem: I think you have been arguing with the wrong philosophers!

Yours sincerely,
David

Special thanks to Dr. David Deutsch, from the Centre for Quantum Computation at the University of Oxford, UK, and Dr. Seth Lloyd, from the Massachusetts Institute of Technology, for their support and the permission to reprint this correspondence.
(Originally published July 9th, 1997 on http://hotwired.lycos.com/synapse/braintennis/97/41/index0a.html.)

It's All the Same Day

"The ancient kingdom of Mesopotamia, which flourished in the region which became Iraq, is what textbooks like to call the birthplace of modern civilization. The Mesopotamians were the first to record their thoughts in writing, the first to divide the day into 24 hours, the first to eat off ceramic plates." [1]

Blame the Mesopotamians. That's what I say. Once there were 24 hours in a day, the idea of a day would forever be locked in place. Weeks would soon follow, then months, years, and so on, for all time. And here we are today. Time would overtake consciousness; an ordering device, but in place of what? An uninterrupted flow of movement and observation? Our freedom?

They were the first to record their thoughts in writing. As if in having been written, put into words on paper, thought is in any way accurately conveyed. Something is always lost. Of this we are well aware. All writing is an act of translation, not always successful, and usually from one language into another. These thoughts are being translated from one language *into its own*, so to speak. To be lost in thought seems impossible to share. Just like now. Tuesday, January 14, 12:47 P.M., Eastern Standard Time. Daylight Savings Time as well. The day ends before it's done. Night comes too soon. And daybreak too. This is due by the 27th, at the very latest. Were deadlines invented in Mesopotamia as well?

Even before calendars, clocks, and watches it was possible to be early or late. You plan to meet someone, arrive before they do, or they before you. You know this without having to check the time. And even if they keep you waiting, if you really want to see them, if you're infatuated or in love, or if it's someone who intends to pay back money borrowed, you don't seem to mind. This is perhaps another reality… where the tyranny of time matters not in the least. Time, like reality, another box to build and be put inside.

Even the automobile, here in America a birthright of sorts – as the ads promise: "It's not just a car, it's your freedom" – is merely a box which conveys us from one compartment to another. For many it's merely a conveyance to work. You punch a time clock at the beginning and end of your shift. The expression "time is money," was it born in this little wall-mounted box? On the way home from work, you listen to the news on the radio. People speaking, symbolically, of course, about the buildup of armed forces in and around the Persian Gulf. You pull into a gas station and think of all the oil underneath ancient Mesopotamia. They ate off ceramic plates and never even knew it was there…

To be able to make the distinction that it is speech, rather than writing, which frees up what passes for accepted reality today, is essential. To speak freely is to inhabit a purely symbolic world, a place where anything can happen. Tell someone you love them, or can't stand them, and whether or not you really do… A pathological liar who's caught in a lie will invariably tell another, sometimes quite believably. This is one way to transcend reality. The con man who wants your wallet, the politician who wants your vote, the boyfriend who wants to be forgiven, the child who wants that toy… shape-shifters, every one of us. Have you ever heard someone in a gallery try to sell a work of art? It's shape-shifting. A kind of performance, and the gallery, like the new car showroom, or the Oval Office, is each in its own way a stage from which to perform. An image is staged and projected in order to alter the space perceived around the moment, around the audience, which may not even be aware that they are an audience.

Artists have always sought to transcend and even transform reality. Think of trompe l'oeil, which translates from the French as "fool the eye." With the increasing use of computers and Photoshop, not only by artists and advertising agencies, but by governments as well, we might think of the term redefined: fool the lie. But isn't there something even more believable about trompe l'oeil? When you look up at a ceiling that has been painted with an expanse of blue sky and fluffy clouds, you know it's the ceiling of the room. You know that the roof hasn't been lifted like a lid from a box. You can see that the clouds and the birds aren't moving. Clouds and birds don't hold that still. And so even if this isn't really the sky above, it has its own undeniable presence. Why is it any less real? When the White House was blown up in the movie *Independence Day*, we knew it was simply a matter of special effects. Back when the movie was in theaters just seven years ago, the audience cheered at the scene. Would they today?

Look at a painting by van Gogh, one for which you might visit the actual place where he painted. Hold a postcard of the painting up to the landscape and what do you see? Or which do you believe? We can lose ourselves in the swirling intensity and luminosity of the painted scene, those sparks of light, stars plugged in like bulbs, or flowers aglow, incandescent. And then you recall that the artist suffered from frontal lobe epilepsy. That the landscape before us may have appeared to him as electric, hallucinatory. Can we ever hope to see this scene as van Gogh had himself? That is, unless we were to experience the heightened vision that accompanies an epileptic episode of the kind to which he was subjected? Of course we always have the painting as our guide.

[1] Deborah Solomon, "Iraq's Cultural Capital," *The New York Times Magazine*, January 5, 2003, p. 15.

The Object "a"

If, today, the art object is found outside or beyond its normal realm, off the wall or extra-terrestrial, this does not mean that it is any less real. It, too, plays its part in the politics of leisure and the entertainment industry. It is even part of the décor of financial markets, bankruptcy, oil wars, and suicide attacks.

If the art object is real, it is not reality, in any case not the whole reality. From the beginning of the last century (or even the end of the one before), art has tried to cut itself from the illusions that represent the illustrations of reality. By being critical of the illustrations of the visual world, art questions the state of things.

Like correct ideas, the art object does not drop from the sky, but by giving up its model and its subject, the art object won its autonomy, even if today this relative autonomy seems, for some, a little problematic.

Instead of being a representation of reality, the art object has become its own reality. By dissolving its meaning into its form, it has become what it is. The object is its own subject: it is the representation of its own representation. The medium is the message. With the loss of its subject, its spectacle and its literature, the irreducibility of its identity can only point to its limits.

We know this. The story has been told before by others who did it better than I ever could have. It's the history of painting from the end of the nineteenth century to the end of the twentieth: the abandonment of perspective, the acknowledgment of the materiality of the support, of its shape, abstraction, and the allover. With its flatness, its frontality, and the two-dimensional quality acknowledged by the edges of the canvas comes an awareness that allows a painting to be seen as a painting. With the liberation of color and form, this autonomy becomes the justification of an artwork's right to exist.

I don't really want to go back to the history of the changes in art's relation to its consumers (the church, the state, etc.) or its connection to society in general, but this new internal dialectic of the art object (which is also a self-criticism) is in fact pointing to the place of its consumption, that is, its use and its value.

If it is not really the beholders who make the work of art (he who makes the work, makes it). They may participate, though, unless the work does it by itself). It is, in any case, others who give (or do not give) value to a work of art. This value is, in the end, an exchange-value and it is this exchange which assures the work of art its surplus-value.

Here, too, there is a history. It is that of the economy. It is the history of the conditions and the methods that allow the preservation of investments and the domination that permits capital accumulation. If the system does not need the art object to manifest its power, it gives the object its permission to exist and art is still one of these ideological apparatuses that participate in strengthening the system. Art plays its part; the market supports art and art supports the market.

The market, where art and the social structure meet, is the foundation of the economy. Its principle is the exchange value, the laws of supply and demand and profit. The market creates a kind of fictional (or not so fictional) competition, which goes further than simple exchange mechanisms and which might very well have some impact on the actual production of a work of art. In the end, is not so much about supply and demand. It is about profit and capital accumulation. The art object is defined by the contradiction between its production and its investment value. The artistic practice is grounded on that contradiction. Even if the market catches up with it, the art practice tries to neutralize this contradiction, which is its way of existing. In the best scenarios, the practice is without illusions, without authorship or ownership. This is in a way what I wanted to say when I made reference to the art object making itself. Perhaps it even exists before being realized. In any case it is always a product of circumstances. It is also more or less a form of ideological appropriation and, as it has been said, passes from one form to another.

We could think that this object is in itself not that interesting, that it does not really exist. What gives the art object its value is its context. The exhibition *Extra Art,* at the CCAC in

California and the ICA in London, showed artists' ephemera, in other words, the products derived from works of art, such as invitations, posters, etc. If this idea were pushed a little further, exhibiting press releases, articles, photographs, or essays, we would point to what, beyond its disappearance, gives value to this object. In fact, this business is the product of a team. The directors of galleries or museums, the curators, the collectors, the assistants, the foundations, and those who pay the bills all participate in the production of the art object. Wasn't, for instance, the original gesture that gave value to the famous bottle-rack its purchase at the BHV in Paris?

Even if I am not often convinced by the exhibitions of those who try to amuse us or by those who forget the conditions that make their work possible, I am well aware that these events and objects could be seen from other points of view and that the art object certainly possesses other dimensions. But here, too, others could talk about it better than I, and I am certainly ready to let them do that. "H E L P," that's what I have said somewhere else, but if that's all there is... then let's sing like Léo Ferré:

"C'EST EXTRA"...

THERE WAS A BAD TREE, A BAD TREE, THAT PEOPLE HATED. THE LEAVES GAVE OFF A FOUL SMELL, AND THE FLOWERS HAD A BITTER STINK. IF YOU GOT TOO CLOSE, YOU VOMITED. THE FRUIT WAS POISON, ONE BITE AND YOU WERE DEAD. EVERYONE REALLY DISLIKED IT. THE BAD TREE STUNK. THEY TALKED ENDLESSLY ABOUT IT; AND DECIDED TO CUT IT DOWN. GET RID OF IT. THEY CHOPPED WITH AXES, AND BARELY MADE A DENT; WEARING BREATHING MASKS, THEY WHACKED AT IT AND WHACKED AT IT, AND NIBBLED AND CHIPPED. OILY POWDER FROM THE SHINY DARK GREEN LEAVES, GOT ON THEIR SKIN, BLISTERED, AND WAS REALLY ITCHY; AND THEY SCRATCHED BLOODY RED. THEY PUT ON PROTECTIVE GEAR WITH OXYGEN, AND WENT AT IT WITH ELECTRIC BUZZ SAWS AND HEAVY EQUIPMENT WORKING 24-HOUR SHIFTS, FINALLY, THEY CUT IT DOWN. EVERYONE WAS VERY HAPPY, AND CELEBRATED THE GREAT VICTORY. A NOBLE DEED, WELL DONE; AND THEY WENT TO BED EXHAUSTED. THE NEXT MORNING, THE BAD TREE HAD GROWN BACK, HAD SPRUNG UP NEW AND BIGGER, AND MORE BEAUTIFUL AND UGLY. IT WAS VERY DISCOURAGING. THEY TALKED A LOT ABOUT IT, AND CUT IT DOWN AGAIN, AND POURED GASOLINE ON THE ROOTS, AND BURNED ALL THE LEAVES AND BRANCHES IN A BIG FIRE. AFTER THE SMOLDERING EMBERS GOT COLD, THE TREE GREW BACK, BIGGER, MORE BAD, AND REALLY GORGEOUS. OTHER PEOPLE HAD BEEN WATCHING FROM THEIR HOUSES, WAITING THEIR TURN. THEY THOUGHT THEMSELVES SMARTER, WITH HIGHER INTELLECTUAL CAPABILITIES, THEY KNEW HOW TO GET RID OF THE TREE. IT WAS A GROWING PLANT, A WOOD TREE THAT GREW IN THE EARTH. THEY INCINERATED IT, BURNED THE ROOTS WITH CHEMICALS, VAPORIZING ACIDS, AND ROBOTIC LASERS; DETONATED ON THE GROUND, BOMBED FROM THE AIR, HIT WITH SMART MISSILES; AND BOMBARDED WITH RADIATION. THEY MADE A FIRE STORM; AND COVERED THE GROUND WITH CONCRETE AND STEEL. THE TREE GREW BACK, MORE FRESH, MORE ELEGANT, EVEN GRACIOUS; AND REALLY UGLY. THE WOOD WAS HARDER, DARKER, MORE SHINY, THICK HOT MUSCLE; AND THE LEAVES, FULL AND LUSH, MOVED LIKE UNDERWATER PLANTS LUXURIOUSLY IN THE BREEZE. EVERYONE WAS VERY DEPRESSED, EXTREMELY DISCOURAGED. IT WAS A CATASTROPHE. THEY HAD MADE FOR THEMSELVES A HELL WORLD. THEY TALKED INCESSANTLY ABOUT IT, AND CAME TO A BIG DECISION. THE MAYOR RESIGNED IN DISGRACE, THOSE, WHO HAD WORKED SO HARD, LEFT, HUMILIATED, DEPARTED, STAYED AWAY, MOVED TO THE OTHER SIDE OF TOWN. THEN, OUT

OF THE BLUE, APPEARED THESE BEAUTIFUL PEOPLE, THEY WERE SIMPLE AND HUMBLE, A LITTLE LIKE PEACOCKS, AND SEEMINGLY WELL-INTENTIONED, WITH A GREAT SENSE OF HUMOR. RADIANTLY RELAXED, OOZING LOVING KINDNESS AND COMPASSION, THEY WALKED RIGHT UP, AND STARTED EATING THE LEAVES. THEY ATE THE LEAVES AND ENJOYED THEM, BECAME HAPPY, AND LAUGHED AND LAUGHED; AND CHOMPED ON MORE LEAVES. YOU COULD TELL THEY REALLY LIKED THE TASTE. ❦ THEY PRESSED THEIR CHEEKS TO THE FLOWERS, BLACK VELVET COATED WITH TRANSMISSION OIL. THEY LICKED THE SWEET JUICES THAT SEEPED FROM THE PETALS. THE POLLEN WAS COAL DUST AND PETROLEUM GAS. BURYING THEIR NOSES, THEY SUCKED IN DEEP BREATHS, EATING THE SMELL, GREAT BLISS. ❦ THEY DISCOVERED THE FRUIT HIDDEN BENEATH THE LEAVES, OVERRIPE MANGOES WITH STICKY EGGPLANT SKIN, HUNG LIKE TESTICLES; AND INSIDE THE FRUIT WAS ROTTING MEAT, LIKE LIVER. THE SPECIAL PEOPLE GOT THEIR FACES INTO THE STINKING SLIME, AND REALLY GOT INTO IT; INHALING WITH THEIR LIPS, AND TEETH, AND TONGUES. THEY LICKED AND DRANK THE TRICK RED JUICE. THE SEEDS, LIKE CABOCHON RUBIES, SEEMED PARTICULARLY POTENT, AND WERE CHEWED WITH GREAT DELIGHT. ❦ THE FRUIT CONTAINED THE FIVE WISDOMS. THE MEN AND WOMEN BECAME LUMINOUS, THEIR SKIN WAS GOLDEN AND THEIR BODIES, ALMOST TRANSPARENT, WERE CLOTHED IN SHIMMERING RAINBOW LIGHTS. ❦ THEY BECAME SLEEPY, YAWNED, AND CURLED UP UNDER THE TREE, AND TOOK A NAP. WHILE THEY SLEPT, MUSIC FILLED THE AIR. LOUNGING AGAINST THE GNARLED TREE TRUNK AND PROTRUDING ROOTS, THEIR HUGE BODIES COLORED RED, YELLOW, BLUE, GREEN, WHITE, RESTED IN GREAT EQUANIMITY, AND RADIATED HUGE COMPASSION. ❦ INSIDE THE TREE WERE THE SECRET HOMES OF MANY DEMI-GODS, HUNGRY GHOSTS, AND EARTH SPIRITS, WHO WERE VERY PLEASED WITH ALL THE POSITIVE ATTENTION BEING PAID TO THEM. AFTER YEARS OF ABUSE, MUTILATION, AND DESTRUCTION, THEY WERE TICKLED; EVEN THOUGH, THEY WERE BEING RAVAGED AND THEIR FLOWERS WRECKED. ❦ AT THE ROOT ENDINGS, THERE WERE JEWELS, DIAMONDS AND EMERALDS AND RUBIES, WHICH WERE STARS IN THE SKY OF THE WORLD BELOW. ❦ THE BEAUTIFUL MEN AND WOMEN WOKE UP, AND NIBBLED ON THE LEAVES, AGAIN; THEY ATE THE LEAVES, LIKE DEER, PAUSING BETWEEN BITES, LOOKING UP AT THE VAST EMPTY SKY. THE LEAVES AND FRUIT INCREASED THEIR CLARITY AND BLISS, AND INTRODUCED THE NATURE OF PRIMORDIALLY PURE WISDOM MIND.

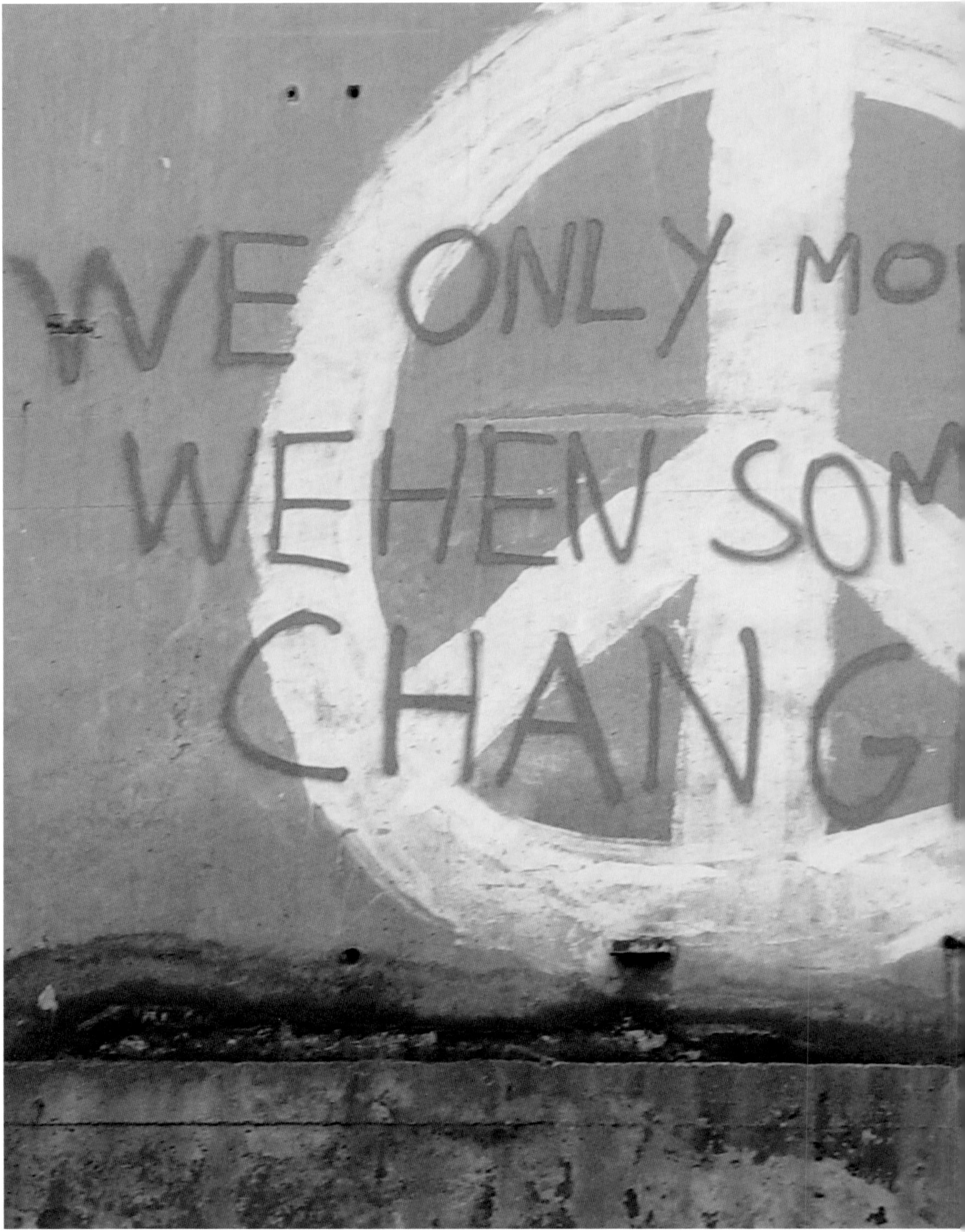
WE ONLY MO
WEHEN SOM
CHANG

THERE WAS THIS DISPLAY IN POSTER RACKS ON A STAIRWAY OF B&W PHOTOS BRAD DUNNING HAD TAKEN OF A PERFORMANCE AT A JUNIOR COLLEGE WITH A MUSCLEMAN AND A SKINNY DANCER DRESSED IN SHINY & MATTE SPIDERMAN COSTUMES POSING WITH WOMEN IN SUPER-STRETCHY COSTUMES WHICH WERE PULLED OFF SCREEN TO ABSTRACT THEIR MODERN DANCE POSES FURTHER. THE ENTRY TO THE SCHOOL WAS SUCH THAT IT LOOKED LIKE A WOMAN'S FACE FROM ONE SPOT AS IT WAS LANDSCAPED IN PERSPECTIVE. THERE WERE TWO NAKED MAN-NEQUINS WITH PURPLE BLOTCHES LYING ON THE FLOOR TYPING. UPSTAIRS I WENT TO A ROOM TO CHANGE & MY MOM SHOWED ME HER ODD-LOOKING PANTSUIT. DAD CAME IN & THEY TALKED ABOUT SOMEBODY I DIDN'T KNOW. I APPROACHED ANOTHER ROOM WITH BENJAMIN. IT HAD A SIGN SAYING THE ALGONQUIN ROUND TABLE HAD MET THERE. INSIDE, THE ROOM HAD ABSO-LUTELY NO FEATURES. IN ANOTHER ROOM IT WAS A SUSPENSE FILM. CLINT EASTWOOD WAS A KILLER WHO USED THREAD TO STRANGLE VICTIMS. A WOMAN WAS LOOKING THROUGH A CRIB FILLED WITH YARN TO MAKE AN ESCAPE ROPE. I SUGGESTED SHE USE THE BLANKETS. AN OLD LADY, WHO'S YARN IT WAS, MADE SUGGESTIONS. THERE WAS A PLASTIC BAG WITH TEETHING RINGS & A KILLER BABY, POSSIBLY IN A PLASTIC BAG.

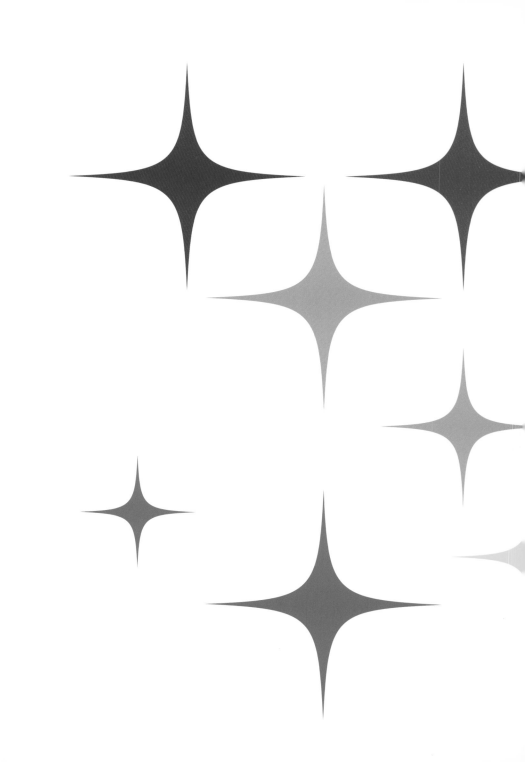

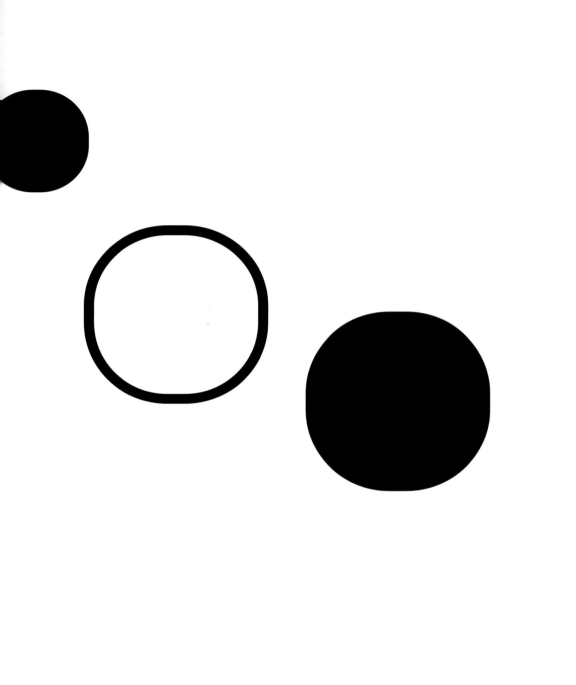

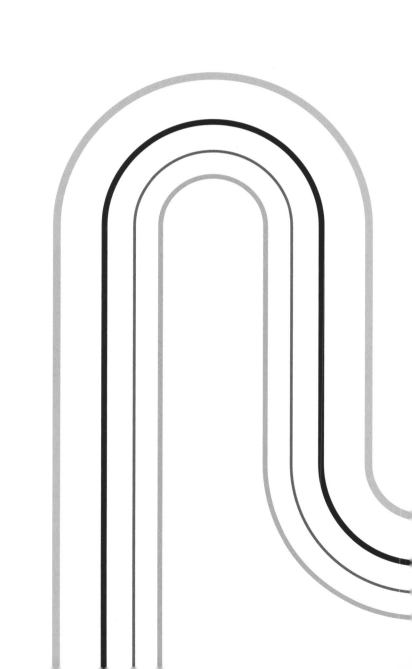

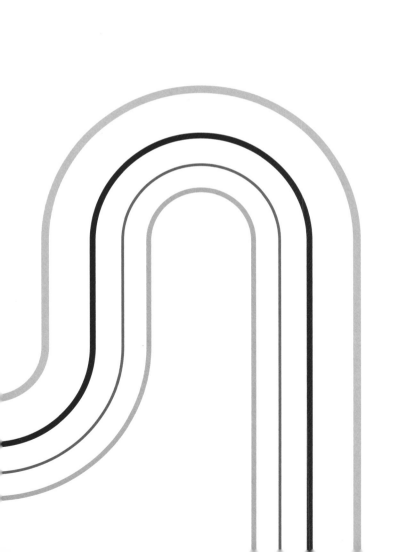

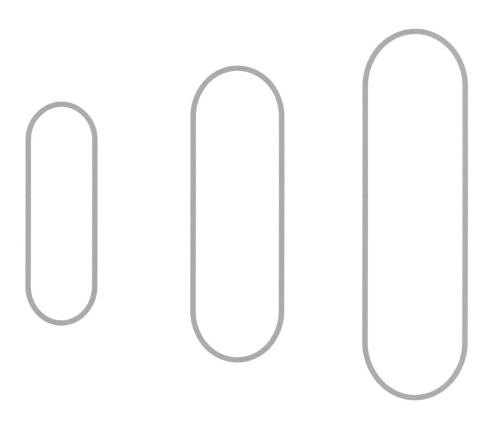

After quietly apprising Scott
of her suspicions, Laura per-
suades Lucky to move back in
for a while. After Brooke leaves
for the office, Beth wonders
aloud why the Forresters are
trying so hard to keep their
daughter from Ridge if there
isn't some truth to what
Brooke claims.

LET
US

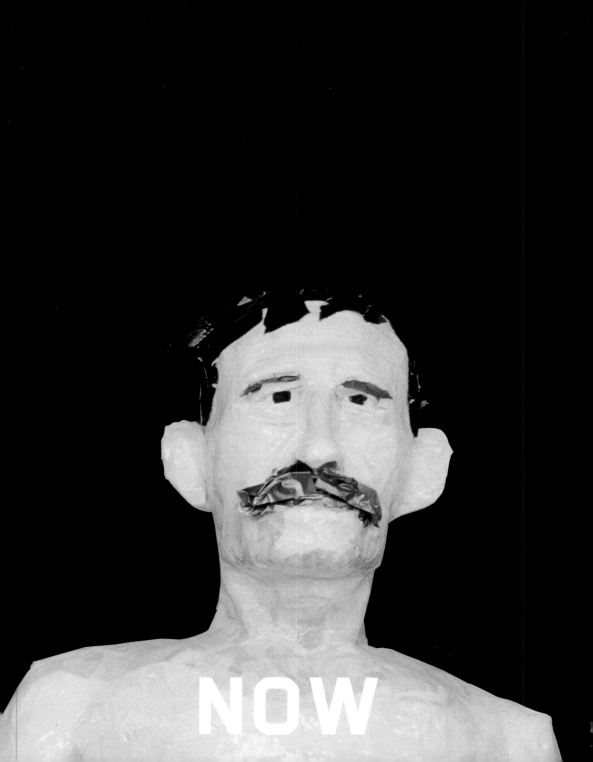

THE GREAT

MEN

RAP
CLASS

hand
xerox

GET THE FEVER

"QUIES"
PARIS

DYNAM
HEAT

NO RULES

again

Chucky

RAINBOW

CRAP
ADDICTS

ATTENTION
FRANCE...
MÉCHANT

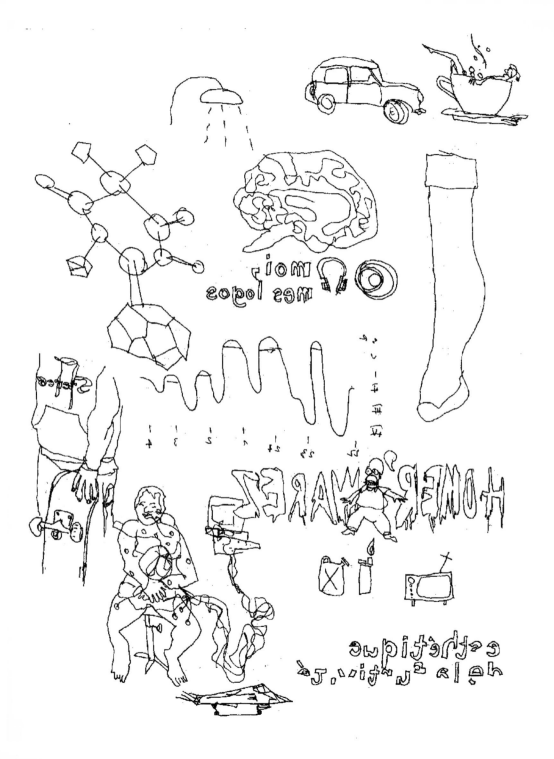

be too lazy to argue

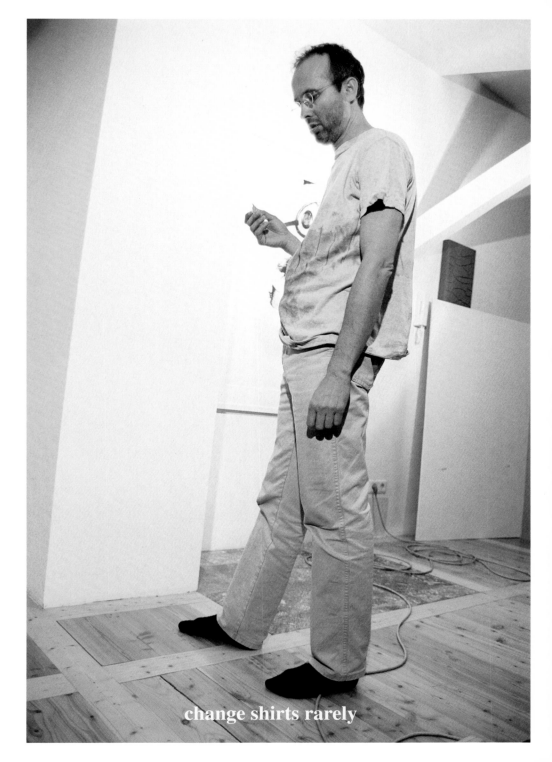

change shirts rarely

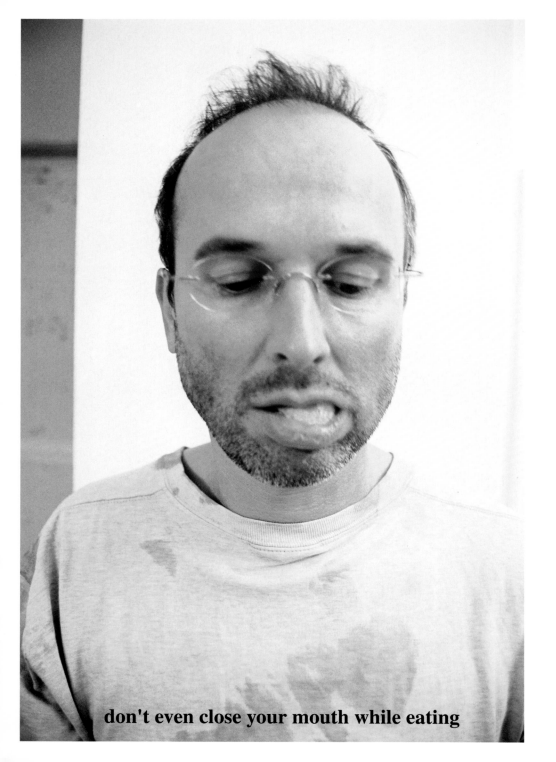

don't even close your mouth while eating

express yourself through yawning

fantasize about nihilism

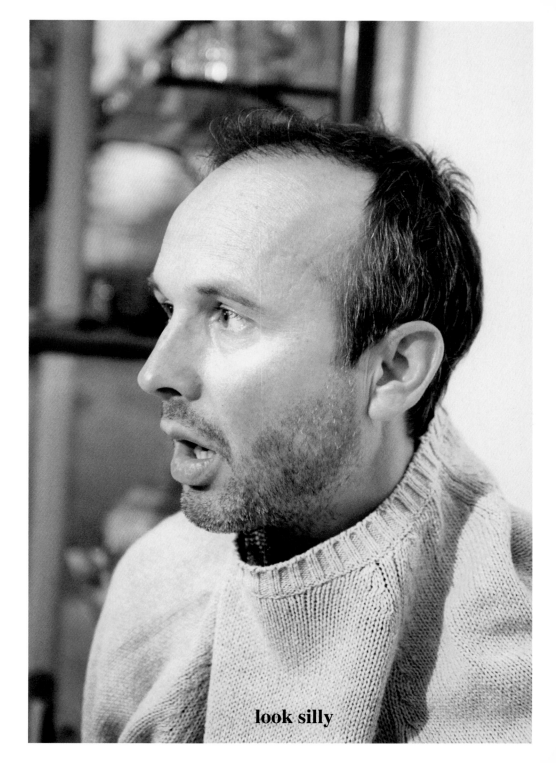

look silly

sleep for two months

smoke a joint before breakfast

stay in your pyjamas all day

take naps on the office toilet

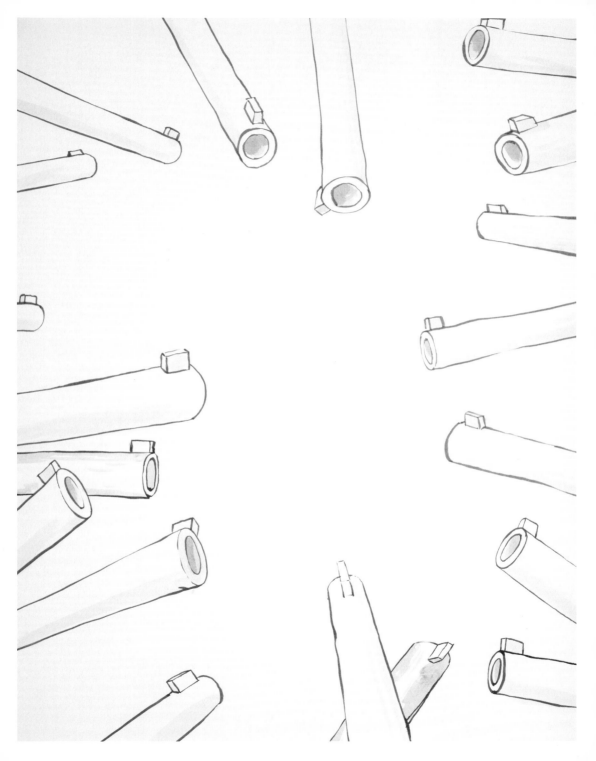

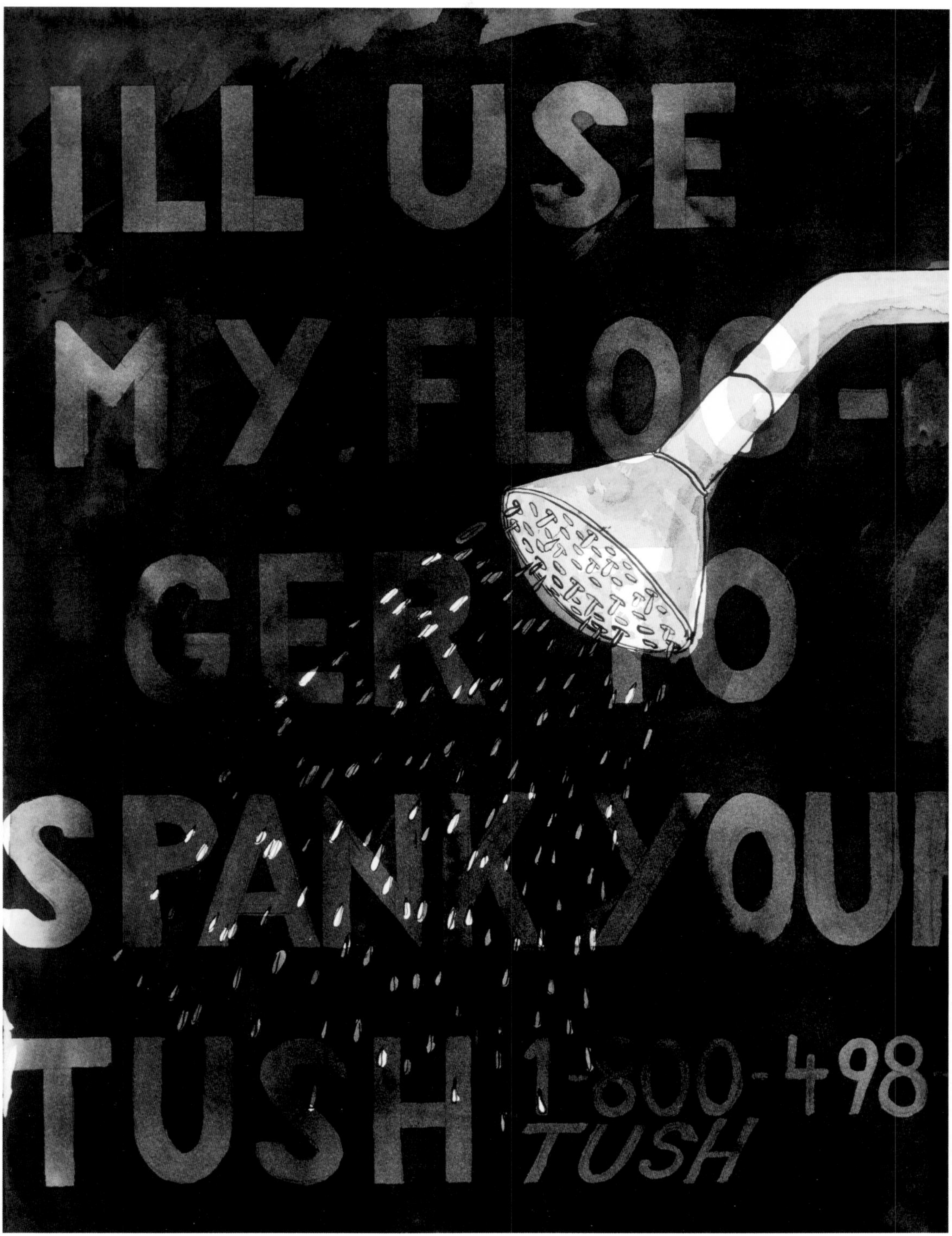
ILL USE
MY FLOG-
GER TO
SPANK YOUR
TUSH
1-800-498-
TUSH

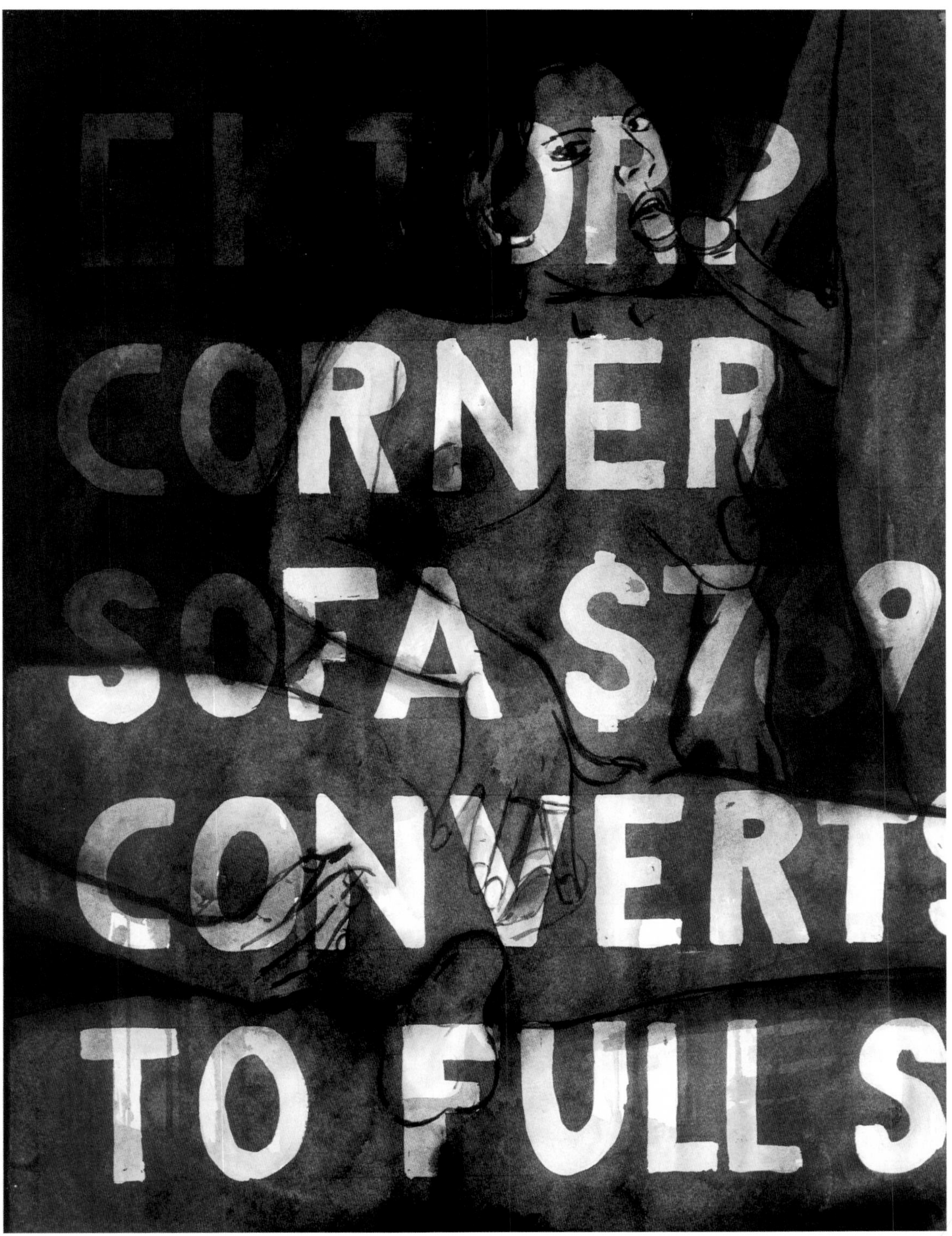
CORNER
SOFA
CONVERT
TO FULL

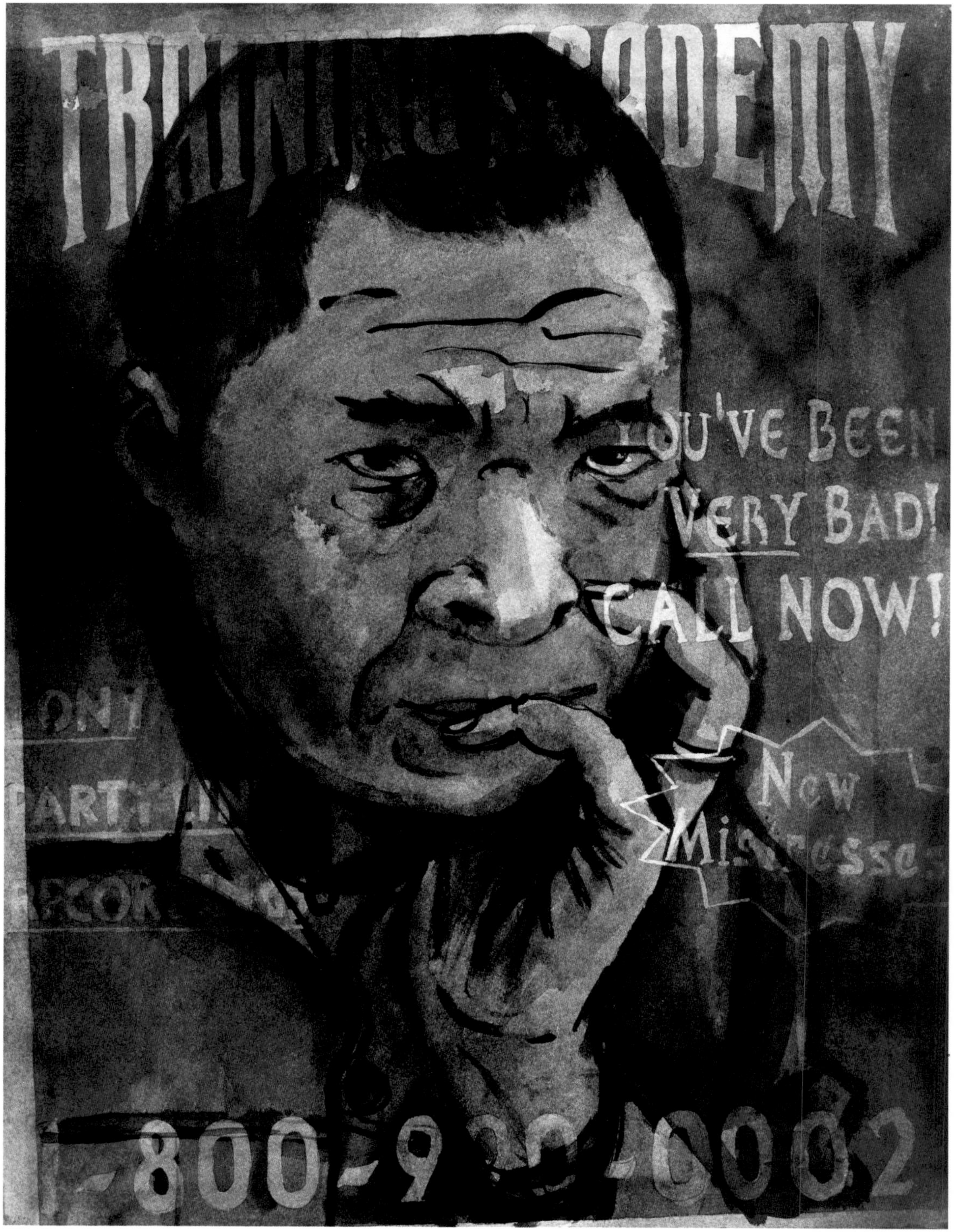
VERY BAD!
CALL NOW!
New

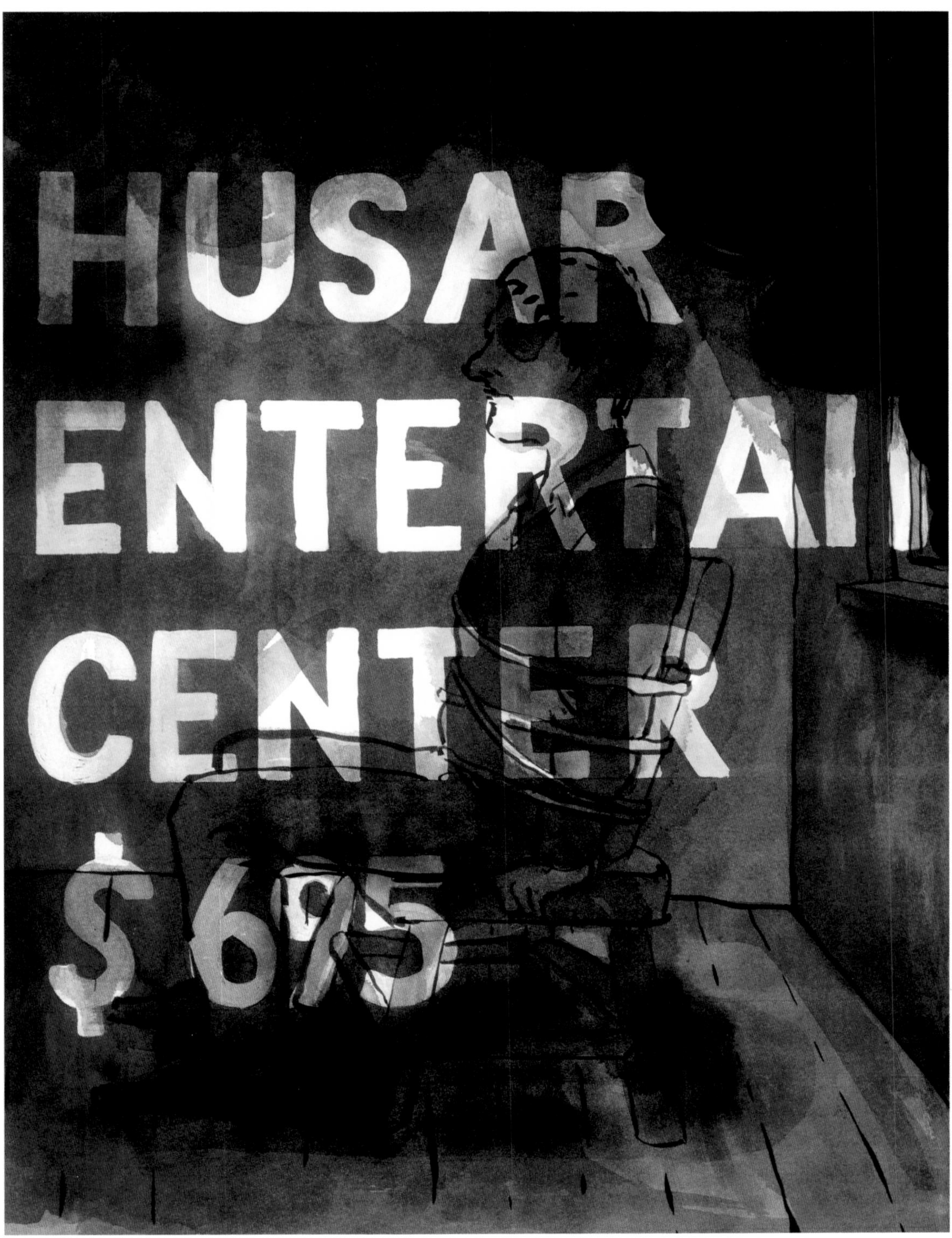
HUSAR
ENTERTAI
CENTER
$695

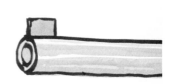

195   197   199   201   203   205

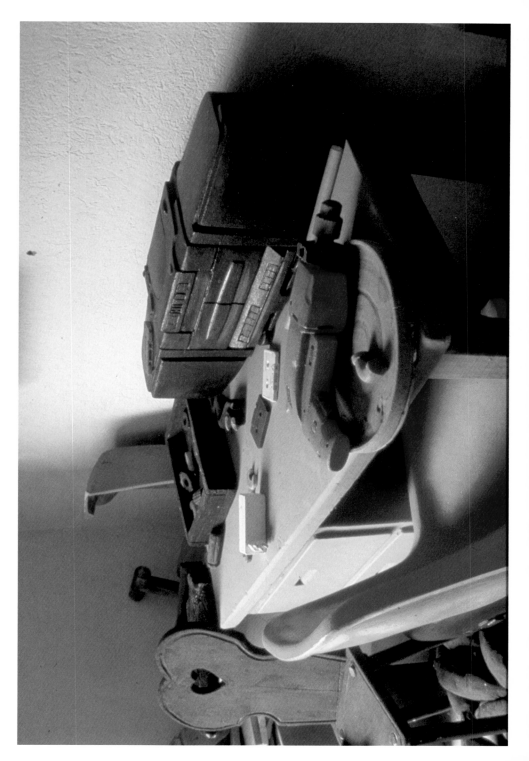

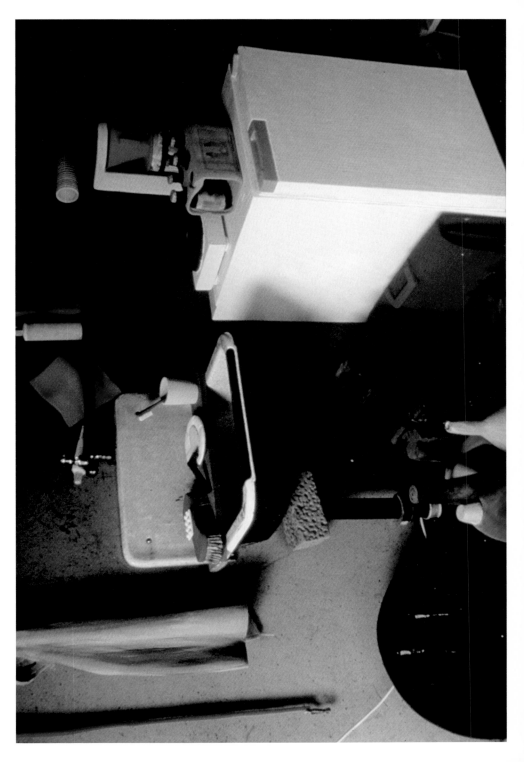

1	2	3	4	5
243	245	247	249	251

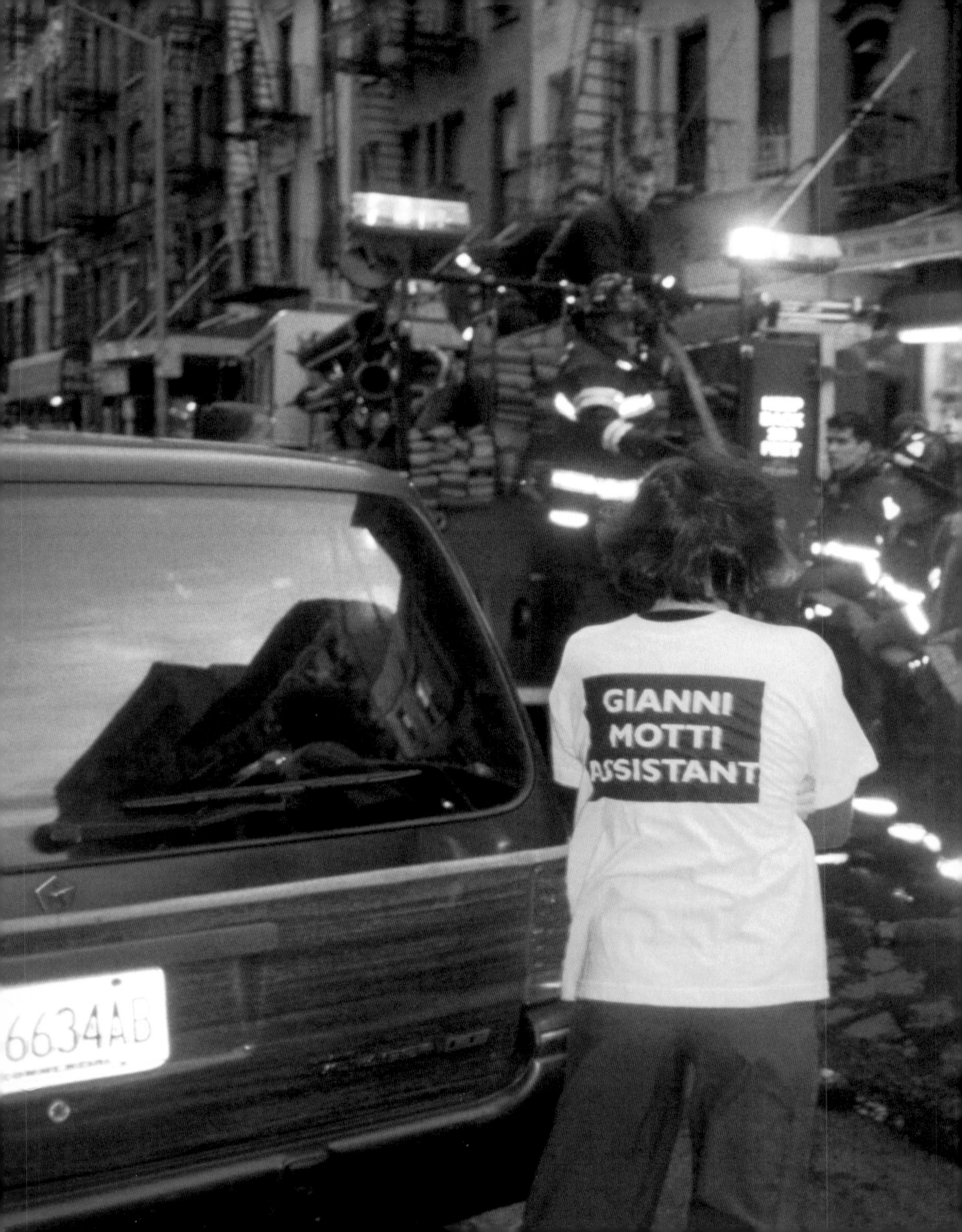
GIANNI
MOTTI
ASSISTANT

Overlook Hotel
July 4th Ball
1921

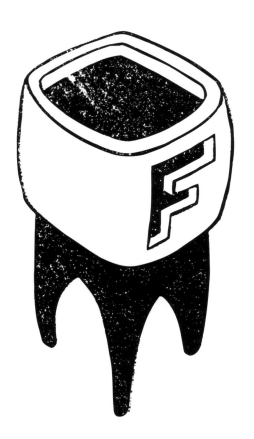

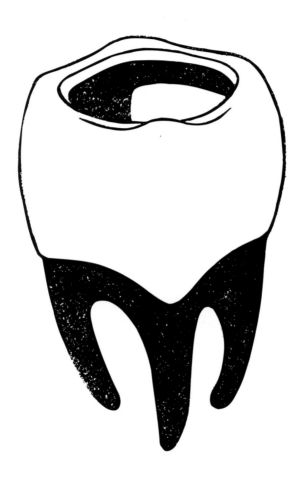

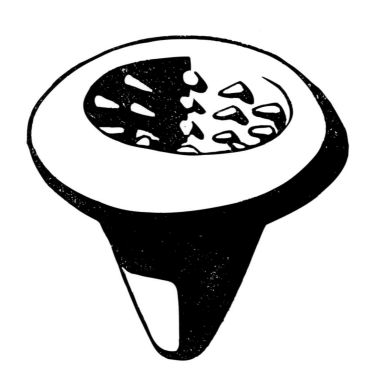

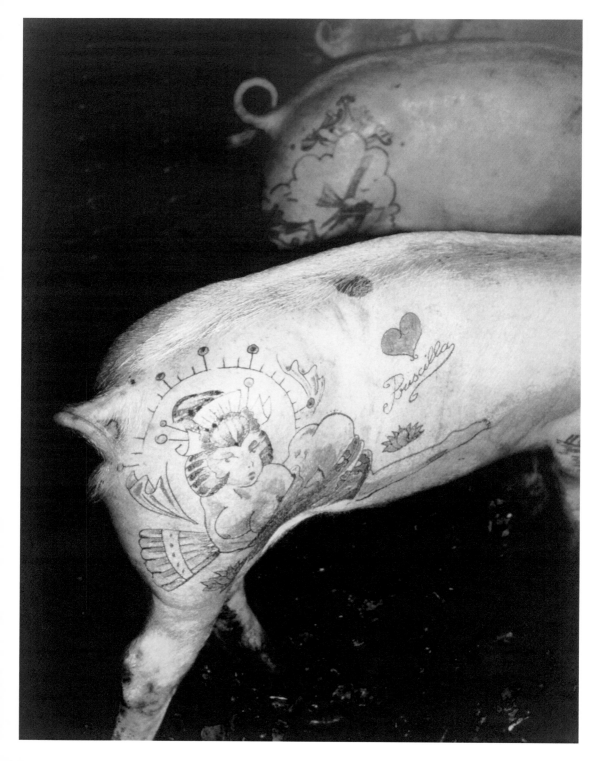

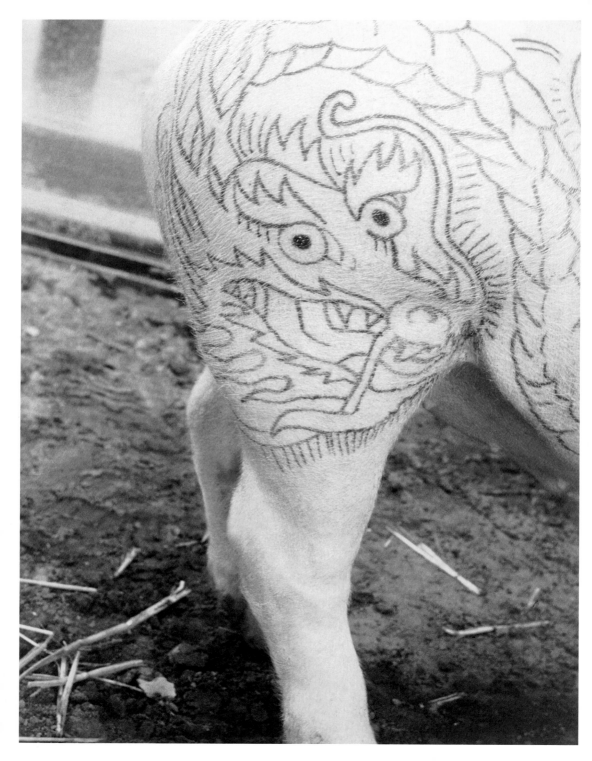

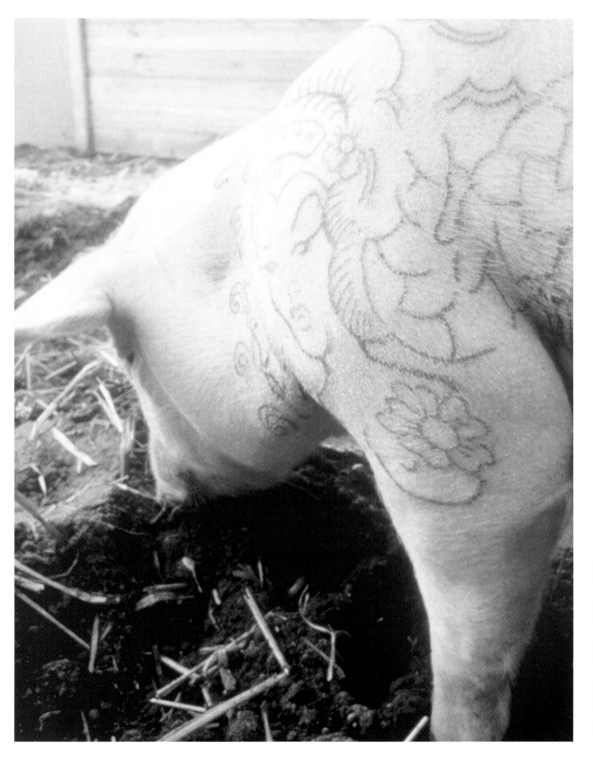

intro (Second Lecture)

one creates new modalities of subjectivity in the ... that an artist creates
forms from the palette" (F. Guattari)
"a subject is the focal ... rance of a process of ..." (A. Badiou)

Goal:
to transform that actual occurance of... into visualities - both physical and mental image
through semi-improvised painting ... learning the art of outside art, outside poetry,
outside music (early Sun Ra, the original Dream Syndicate, Morton Feldman, Giancinto
Salvatore ......)

In that process we can take instructions from all kinds of sources (S. Zizek, ... Lacan,
A. Badiou, G. I. Gurdjieff) and (see reading list)

What the proper historical stance (as opposed to historicism) "relativizes" is not the
past, but paradoxically the present itself ... our present itself is conceived not only as
outcome of what actually happened in the past, but also the unrealized potential of the
future that were contained in the past. We have to conceive ourselves as the
materialization of the ghost of past generations. As the ... in which these past
generations retroactively resolve their deadlock... (A. Badiou was present) ... and
and as in politics, take refuge in ... a dimension of our interaction ... order ... to the
deadlock.

Can we do ... art in ... way ... can we ... play ... an artificial ... institute ...
progress ...
... ... more about that and its practical implications?

Since this is a painting workshop there will be a focus on painting ... or ...
... made discussion and use of additional media in your workdays ...

Topic:
What is our practice about? (besides ... ... material content ...
imagination of ... petition exhibit ... ...
a psychic ... energy ... that deals in in... ...
liberation of ... imagin ... ... context be a sub-
text ...
artist produces ... should event ...
artist as ... spirit at ... a ... deranged ... face ... vanishing ana-
chronist because we're being a spec ... catch ... and we want ...
think about ... abstract universal ... opposes the ... state socialism
... thinking ... rules should be specific (limited ...) for practicing a temporary
... ...on of its corporate hierarchy
... and antisymmetric elements of imagination ... and examples ... past art
... about analytical aggression in painting ... ...
... future ... or ... accelerate ... ...

Jutta and I had a discussion about failed paintings. Maybe the color wasn't right or they were fucked up in some way (physically, ideologically or by situation). Our solution was to save them by blacking them out, canceling the image/object. A positive/negative, deconstruct to reconstruct, chaos to order to chaos, (like cities, civilizations, planets, suns, universes) an eternal truth. We decided to show these re-claimed paintings and dedicate the show to George Grosz's "DeathDada" caught in the flux between dissonance and consonance. - S.P.

All NEW
PROPOSAL FOR A PAINTING-PROJECT that deals with Painting as a contender for aggressive analysis and accelerated formalism!

BLACK BONDS
is a 2-person exhibition by Jutta Koether and Steven Parrino

Black is the color of NY. Black is the color of fashion. Black sucks. Black is the color of a cover-up of a materialistic mess. We paint over works that were found, dismissed, or had been sent back to us by art-dealers. Work, that didn't make it, the work that caused black moods, anger, misery, and enforced rethinking of enlightening. Color black, a symbol for rough trading. Black is the failure of failure.
So are our paintings. They are mental-events. Self-alienating spirits at work. They are extremists; they are deranged drills for a vanishing anti-market behaviors. Here is the Painting Liberation Army! Causing deliberate Blackouts. We feel a necessity to practice a temporary brutal formalism. It's Black. Black is the color of Painting. Our project also includes sessions of Black-Out-Sound (this is the directly collaborative part of the show), musical performances, that ideally will take place right there in the same space, where the paintings will be have been installed beautifully. From there the Black Stuff will scream: It was us who did it, not you! The call it energetic pessimism!
NY-2000

INTERMISSED
Now, what am I doing here?
We are in the gray zone, confronted with a re-actualized painting (painting), discovering that it (painting) still "speaks to us"? Painting practiced as outside art as in outside music (Sun Ra, Sonic Youth, the original Dream Syndicate, Morton Feldman, K Salvatore... etc.). It is a semi-improvisational painting, abstracted, but with a motive (could be... eagle, gothic emblem, bat, or a Milton Avery-bird) tumbling down. Jewellified there is an option for studying the process carefully, closely (w/a magnifying sheets attached to painting). - J.K.

A field presenting the psychic economy, which does us in. A field that is about looking, a field that is about digging. Made in layered sessions in NYC, turbulent dives from art into everyday life, live conversations, special visual encounters. Call it process or social substance, it's a leap of faux n'faith.

Paraphrasing Slavoj Zizek in the process I would like to describe this work as painting containing the notion of our abyss of freedom, some analytical aggression, and the "dimension of universality as the true opposite of capitalist globalism"!

We know "the universally accepted point of reference is missing, we are thrown into a process of radically open and unending symbolic (re)negotiation and (re)invention". But then:

Painting as a site, that provides us symbolically with the ground on which we thrive, the all-is-already-always-there-stuff (Hail Hegel!). And the artist is both its stumbler and accelerator! (Hail Royal Trux! Veterans Of Disorder) And out of that emerges an imagination/subject with a disruptive, anti-synthetic visuality.

"No trouble no energy,no energy no life"
"Ladies of the Rope"
"Seeking the Extreme"
"Event Mental" - J.K.

THE DISORDER OF BLACK MATTER
a personal lament and high mannerist tendencies in Modernism (of late).
It may sound strange to say, but I still think that painting should strive toward the highest quality. Painting can be beautiful and vital (maybe more now since the art world is based on or shall I say de-based by the ordinary on a colossal scale and art as tourism "the revenge of Pop"). I have personal reasons for my repainting of certain paintings (BLACK). Reclaiming them like so much dead... bringing them power, facing my newly risen zombie Abstraction no longer as a pure formalism. I want to be profoundly touched by art, by life. I came to painting at the time of its death, not to breath it's last breath, but to caress its lifelessness. The necromancer of the Pieta, Pollock's' "One" timed with the birth of a synthetic star. 1958. Black Paintings. Death & Disasters. Modernism at its most powerful before the pointless circus begins. The dust clears (just barely) and I stand in my own graveyard. I hear the constant din of Black Noise.

"Self-mutilation Bootleg"
"Existential Trap for Speed-freaks"
"Corpse Grinders" - S.P.

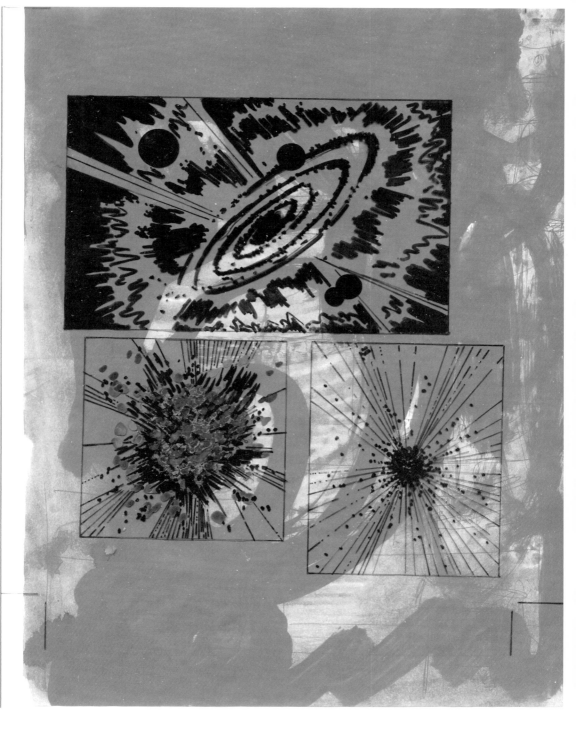

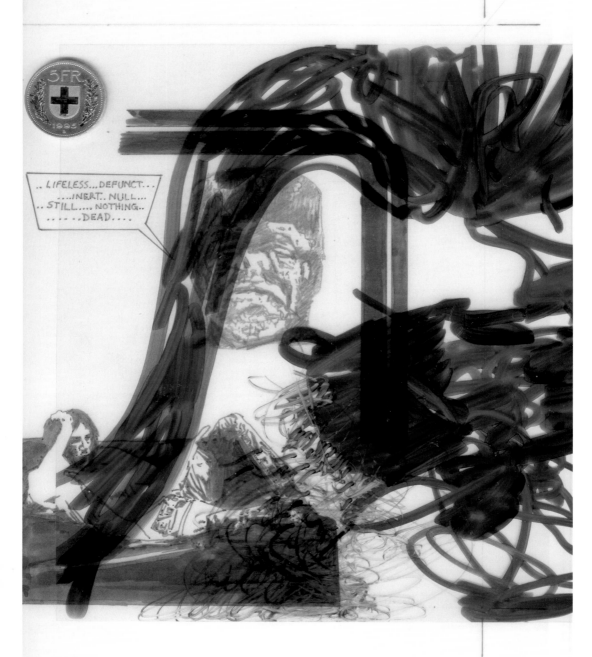

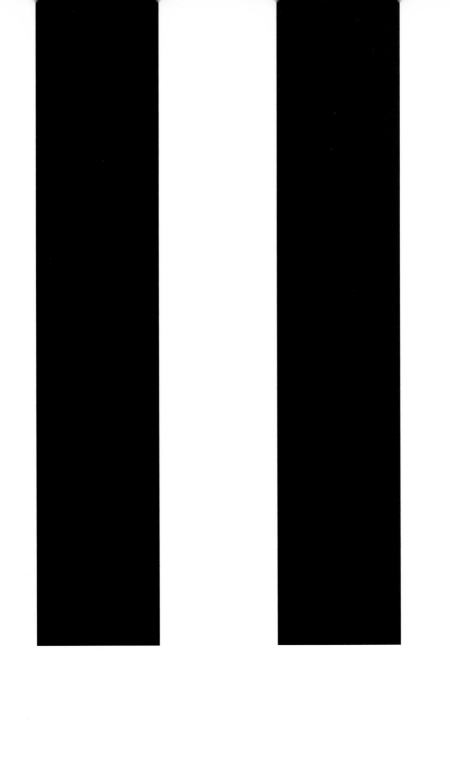

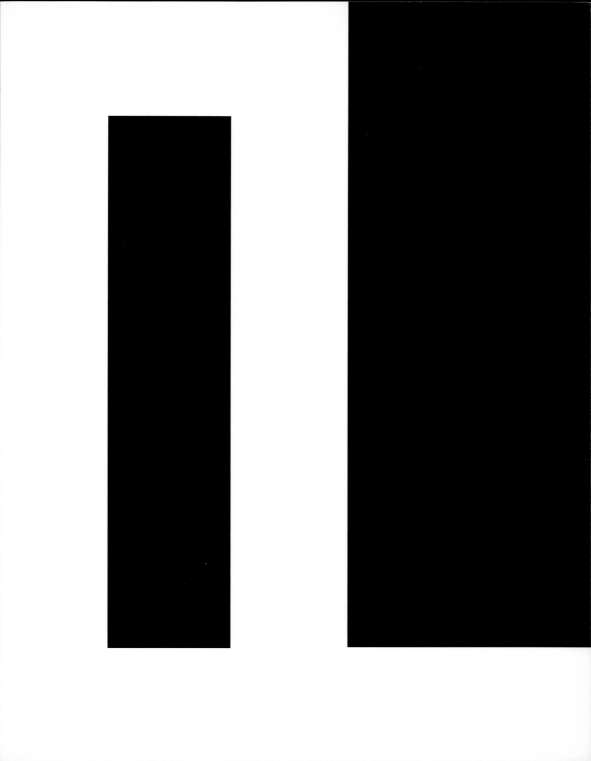

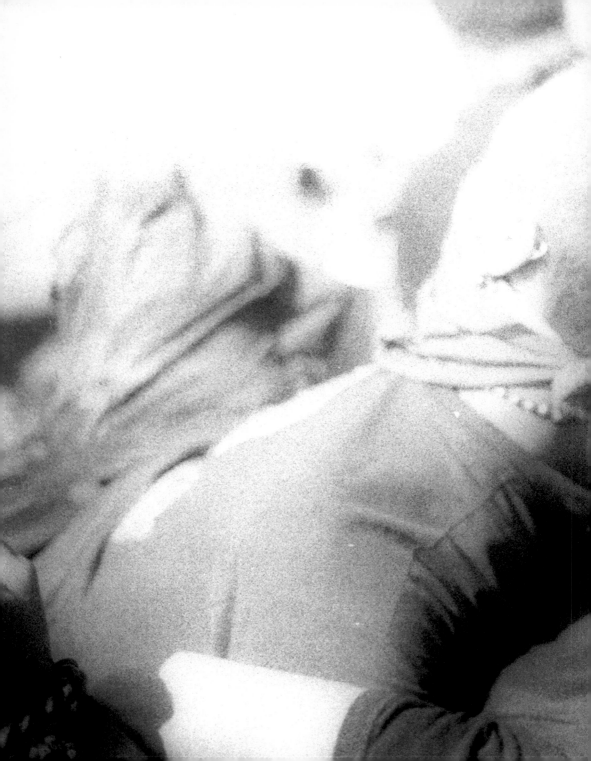

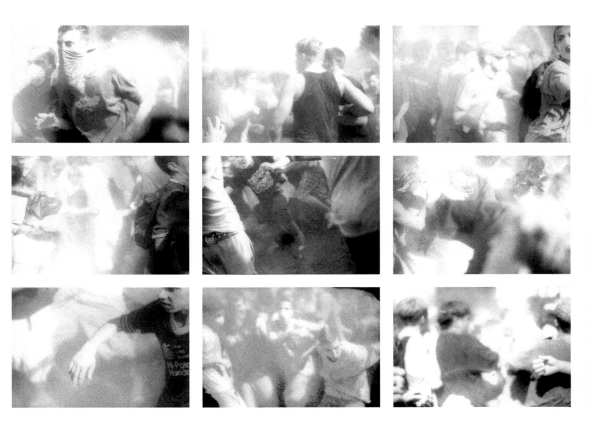

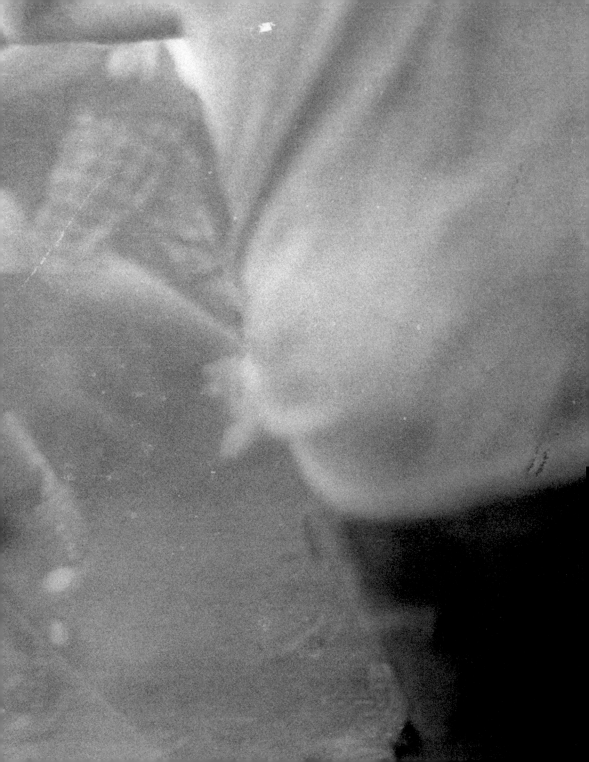

EXTRA

Never get out of the boat. Absolutely goddamn right.
Unless you were going all the way.

Captain Willard, Apocalypse Now

Zusammenfassung der früheren Episoden

Mike Tyson bildet nicht nur eine außergewöhnliche Erscheinung in der Geschichte des Boxens, er liefert auch einen Schlüssel zum Verständnis eines ganzen Kunstbereichs von heute. Die Kraft und vor allem die Schnelligkeit seiner Schläge zwingen den Fernseh-zuschauer, sich Gedanken über die Begriffe *Stealth*[1] und *Fotogenität* zu machen, die im Erscheinungsbild seiner Kämpfe wahrnehmbar werden. Eines meiner Lieblingsvideos zeichnet "Die besten K.O.s von Mike Tyson" nach. Jedesmal wenn ich den glücklosen Herausforderer zusammenbrechen sehe, bin ich verblüfft, dass Tysons Faustschlag unsichtbar bleibt. Er ist so schnell, dass er sich in den Stealth-Bereich verflüchtigt[2], und so brutal, dass er fotogen wird. Ich lasse die Szene in Zeitlupe durchlaufen, sehe Tyson zum Angriff ausholen, dann, übergangslos, seine eiserne Faust dem Gegner ins Gesicht schmettern, der wie ein nasser Sack zu Boden geht. Weder die Zuschauer noch ein-leuchtenderweise der Gegner haben den Schlag in seiner Gänze (seiner Zeitdauer, seiner Verlaufsbahn) gesehen. Wenn der Schlag jedoch unsichtbar ist, auf welche Weise schreibt er sich dann in unsere Wirklichkeit ein, und wie kann er derart spektakulär werden? Die Faszination, die Tyson auf die gewöhnlichen Sterblichen ausübt, beruht auf dieser para-doxen Doppelgegebenheit von Stealth und Fotogenität. Nun sind aber seit einigen Jahren diese beiden Begriffe zu einem Schlüsselkonzept geworden, das auf die neuen Darstel-lungscodes und Realitätskonstruktionen, die viele aktuelle Künstler ins Werk setzen, ein erhellendes Licht wirft.

Episode 14
BOXKAMPF, STEALTH, APOKALYPSE,
VERGEWALTIGUNG UND ZEITGENÖSSISCHE KUNST

ZWISCHEN STEALTH UND DEM FOTOGENEN

Man kann nicht genug betonen, dass das Stealth-Prinzip zwar von den Militärs stammt und unter ihrem Regiment steht, aber in die Welt der Kunst eingebrochen ist wie eine Schockwelle. Stealth hat nichts mit Tarnung zu tun. Ziel der Tarnung ist das Verbergen. Ein getarntes Objekt nimmt bestimmte Formen und Farben an, durch die es nicht unsichtbar werden, aber unbemerkt bleiben kann. Es verkleidet sich, versteckt sich. Man hat es hier mit einer überkommenen Jagdtechnik zu tun, einer uralten Kriegspraxis. Definitiv zum angesagten Fashionstandard geworden (selbst wenn manche Armeen ob seiner Billigkeit noch auf dieses althergebrachte Verfahren zurückgreifen), verkörpert die Tarnung in den Augen der Krieger von heute allerdings eine Duckmäusermethode. Über-lassen wir dem gewöhnlichen Soldatenvolk sein Spiel "du versteckst dich in einer Höhle, und ich werf möglichst viele Bomben auf dich ab". Auch wer etwa in einem Straßenkampf auf den unglücklichen Gedanken kommt, sich zu verstecken, ist ein Feigling, ein Schwäch-ling, ein Waschlappen.

Als etwas ganz anderes erweist sich das Stealth-Objekt. Seine Haupteigenschaft besteht darin, alle optischen Signaturen zu sprengen; es lenkt die Signale um, zertrümmert oder absorbiert sie. Es mutiert, täuscht vor. Es verbirgt sich nicht, sondern unterläuft die sig-nalgeleiteten Aufklärungstechniken. Dabei kann das Stealth-Objekt für das bloße Auge durchaus vollkommen sichtbar bleiben. Stealth (mangelnde Sichtbarkeit) kann sich blitz-artig ins genaue Gegenteil verwandeln: ins Fotogene (überdeutliche Sichtbarkeit). Ein Stealth-Bomber zum Beispiel entzieht sich der Sicht auf den Radarschirmen. Für derlei Messinstrumente ist er unsichtbar, kommt er nicht vor. Dabei erkennt das menschliche Auge ihn mühelos. Und sobald er sichtbar ist, wird er nicht nur verwundbar, sondern vor allem auch hyper-spektakulär. Dann ist er fotogen. Unsichtbar *und* hyper-spektakulär, im Stealth-Bereich *und* fotogen – ein solches Objekt bietet ein absolut verblüffendes Paradox, das der Aufmerksamkeit der Künstler nicht entgangen ist.

TIER DER APOKALYPSE

In diesem Sinne ist Mike Tyson ein Musterfall. Einerseits ist er das Wesen, das imstande ist, seinen Gegner mit einem unsichtbaren Schlag niederzustrecken (der aus dem

Nirgendwo zu kommen scheint, um seinen Schwung auf dem Gesicht des Widersachers zu beenden), anderseits verkörpert er zugleich ein auf der Hyper-Spektakularität des Ereignisses fußendes Modell. Am Fernseher gesehen, tauchen seine Schläge aus dem Nichts auf, offenbar aus jener unsichtbaren Spanne des Zwischenraums, der 24 Bilder pro Sekunde jeweils miteinander verbindet und der *in extenso* den Film als unsere Wirklichkeit ausformt.

Das Paradox des Stealth-Objekts bleibt bei Tyson vollständig erhalten. Seine Schläge entgehen der Aufmerksamkeit des Kathodensignals (visuell existieren sie nicht). Gleichzeitig aber gehört das, was zu sehen ist, in den Bereich des Hyper-Spektakulären und zeugt von einem Überschuss des Sichtbaren. Ein unverwundbarer Mann mit seinem Gegner, der am Boden liegt. Die Wirkung dieses packenden Bildes wird von der Persönlichkeit des Boxers vervielfacht - ein der Vergewaltigung angeklagter Champion, der auf jedwede Selbstbeherrschung verzichtet und alles auf seinem Weg plattmacht, ob es der Autofahrer ist, der ihm die Vorfahrt nimmt, Miss Black America, die nicht rechtzeitig niederkniet, der Ringrichter, der das Massaker zu beenden versucht, oder, kürzlich, der Leibwächter seines künftigen Gegners, der eine suspekt erscheinende Gebärde andeutet. Und wenn er seinen Gegner nicht zerschmettert, beißt Tyson wild auf ihn ein und handelt damit auf eine Weise, die dem Kannibalismus nicht weniger nahesteht als einer Kampftechnik.

Mike Tyson ist die zeitgenössische Inkarnation des Tiers der Apokalypse. "[Er] ist zweifellos derjenige, für den ihn alle halten. Der Böse. Das Tier. Der Durchgeknallte. Aber im Unterschied zu denen, die ihn so nennen, ist er wenigstens kein Heuchler. Er ist genau der, als den man ihn will. (...) Er ist wegen Vergewaltigung ins Gefängnis gewandert. Er hat Gegner zu Boden geschlagen. Einem anderen hat er vorsätzlich den Arm zu brechen versucht. (...) Seit zehn Jahren ist er weniger Boxer als Scheusal. Er ist eine potentielle Katastrophe, ein totaler und programmierter Untergang, für den ihr alle zu zahlen bereit seid, damit ihr dabei seid, wenn er sich produziert, um euch Angst einzujagen an dem Tag, an dem es passiert. [Seine Kämpfe] begeistern die Öffentlichkeit, weil es sich um einen Horrorfilm mit dem besten Darsteller in diesem Fach handelt."[3]

DER VERGEWALTIGTE VERGEWALTIGER

Auch wenn derartiges Verhalten dem Boxer Weltruhm sichert, weiß Mike Tyson, dass er nur gut daran täte, sich zartfühlender aufzuführen. Das würde ihm das Gefängnis ersparen, die einhellige Verdammung der Medien und den Bannfluch der Boxgemeinde. Irgendwo sähe er sich gern allein wegen seiner Faustkämpferqualitäten geliebt und anerkannt. Doch im Grunde seiner selbst drängt ihn immer diese Stimme, nicht auf die Sirenen des sozial Korrekten zu hören, sondern seinem Image als diabolischer Exterminator entsprechend zu handeln. Und er kämpft. Er kämpft so lang er kann darum, sich den Standards einer zivilisierten Gesellschaft anzupassen, wo der Mann die Frau achtet, ein Autofahrer dem entgegenkommenden eine freundliche Geste entbietet, der Sportsmann seinem mutigen Gegner die Hand drückt. Eine Idealgesellschaft, definiert durch herzliches Gemeinschaftsgefühl, unterschiedslosen Respekt und ständiges Lächeln.

Um sich in sie einzufügen, ist Iron Mike zu allen Opfern bereit. Er stopft sich mit Antidepressiva voll. Er heiratet die reizende Sarah Tyson, die das Educational Department von Santa Fe als vorzügliche Kunststudentin schildert, Expertin in Pastell, Ölmalerei und Gastronomie.[4] Er tritt sogar zum Islam über, ein obligatorischer Weg, wenn man ein schwarzer Boxer ist und über sechs Monate lang im Gefängnis sitzt. Er kämpft, doch jedesmal wenn er sich der gesellschaftlichen Anerkennung annähert ("Mensch Mike, ist ja gut, wir verzeihen dir! Mike, ein Lächeln für den Mann von der Presse! Mike, sag, dass du dieses Joghurt magst. Hier unterschreiben, Mike, unten rechts!"), ertönt eine Stimme und drängt ihn, all die unternommenen Anstrengungen zu sabotieren. ("Nein, Mike, lass dich nicht von dieser sozialen Lauheit verhexen, verweigere dieses leisetreterische Image vom "guten Black", der die Integration in die Welt der Weißen geschafft hat. Mike, du bist nicht Colin Powell, du bist der Schrecken der Straßen, der Albtraum der Ladies, der Bin Laden des Boxkampfs! Mike, greif an!")

Mike ist in der Zwickmühle. Ob er sich für den Aufstieg in die Höhen des sozial Korrekten entscheidet oder für ein Abtauchen in den Kessel der Apokalypse, das Ergebnis erweist sich stets als gleichermaßen verhängnisvoll. Wie immer seine Wahl ausfällt, eine Hälfte seines Wesens vergewaltigt die andere. In ständiger Überwerfung mit sich selbst, zerreißt es ihm die Seele, und sie tobt sich an seinen Gegnern aus, an seiner Frau oder jedem anderen Menschen, der ihm über den Weg läuft. Vom Stealth bis zur Fotogenität – Mike Tyson gleitet auf der Oberfläche des Realen, ohne es greifen, anhalten zu können, um sein Maß zu nehmen. Er versucht, dieses Reale, das sich ihm entzieht, zu durchschlagen, indem er seine Umgebung niederschlägt. Doch wie in jenem Spiel, in dem man auf Murmeltiere haut, die daraufhin verschwinden, um aus einem anderen Loch wieder aufzutauchen, dringt das Reale immer wieder an die Oberfläche. Je mehr Mike ins Alter kommt, desto mehr entfernt er sich von dem modernistischen Modell, dem zufolge man ihn (so wie andere Sportler oder Künstler) leicht für einen unbesiegbaren Ritter halten konnte, begabt mit einer von einem anderen Planeten gekommenen Macht, wie ein Außerirdischer, der unfreiwillig das Aussehen eines Menschen angenommen hätte, aber fest entschlossen wäre, dem Planeten Erde zu zeigen, dass er KEIN Mensch ist und uns alle mit Mann und Maus vernichten wird. Nun richten aber diese Mächte nichts gegen den Effekt des Realen aus. Am Ende steht der Gegner wieder auf, um Mike auf die Matte oder ins Gefängnis zu befördern. Sein gesamtes Leben wechselt zwischen diesen beiden Zuständen: dem *Über-Menschen*, dem *Alien* (eine Figur, die er zu Anfang wirklich verkörpert hat, die aber unweigerlich zur "Geschichte", ja "Legende" geworden ist), und dem *Unter-Menschen*, einer allseits ausgebeuteten Leidensfigur, einem flüchtigen (*furtif*) Schatten auf der Suche nach einer Seele. Mike Tysons Geschichte ließe sich in einem Filmtitel zusammenfassen: "Das fabelhafte Schicksal des vergewaltigten Vergewaltigers". Diese Analogie zur Vergewaltigung erlaubt uns eine Rückkehr zu den weiter oben entwickelten Begriffen Stealth und Fotogenität. Denn wenn ein gleichermaßen abwesendes und übersichtbares Objekt die Eigenheit hat, seine optische Signatur zu sprengen und die Aufklärungssysteme zu unterlaufen, so ist sein Ziel letzten Endes die Vergewaltigung eines Territoriums, das Eindringen in eine Zone mit allen Mitteln, seien sie soft, indirekt, unsichtbar, täuschend, also mittels Stealth, oder frontal, roh, spektakulär und fotogen. Die Künstler von heute artikulieren ihre Praxis auf der Grundlage von Modellen, die von solchen Strategien inspiriert sind. Sie entwickeln Infiltrationstaktiken, spinnen eine Vielzahl von Netzen und verdrehen die Regeln der Sichtbarkeit. Sie stellen sich nicht mehr als

romantische Helden gegen den Rest der Welt dar, wie John Waynes auf weißen Pferden. Sie gleiten auf der Oberfläche der Landschaft. Im Bewusstsein, dass das Reale kein zu erschließendes Gebiet mehr ist, sondern eher ein klimatisierter Supermarkt mit einem Überangebot an Information, ein Transitort, an dem Bewegung unumgänglich ist, stellen sie ihre Reisegeschwindigkeit absichtlich auf die ihres Flurnachbarn ein. Sie infiltrieren die Masse der von der Banalität ihrer alltäglichen Verrichtungen anästhesierten Pendler. Sie machen sich ein Prinzip ständiger Mobilität zu eigen und scheinen jene "Gleich-gültigkeit" zu bestätigen, "von der die Realität fortan befallen ist"[5]. Doch wenn sie Anstalten machen, innezuhalten, scheint die Wirklichkeit aus den Fugen geraten. Eine – für gewöhnlich unsichtbare – Kleinigkeit nimmt eine spektakuläre Dimension an. Sie wird fotogen. Neue Paradigmen tauchen auf… Die Künstler sind ohne Vorwarnung in unser Deutungssystem eingebrochen.

Dämonisch und mediatisch zugleich, handeln sie vor aller Augen, aber im Zwischenraum, in einer unaufhörlich sich entfaltenden Falte, in einem ständigen Transit, der ihre Aktionen gleichzeitig unsichtbar und hyper-spektakulär, anonym und skandalös werden lässt.

Episode 15
ENTGLEITEN

DER TOURIST UND DER AUSSERIRDISCHE

Wenn Kunstzentren oder Galerien ihn einladen, am Abend der Vernissage "das Ereignis zu gestalten", hütet Gianni Motti sich vor persönlichen Performances jedwelcher Art. Nein, er verschwindet und überlässt seinen Platz den Akteuren der Realität. Am 27. September 1997 entführt er in Genf den Bus einer japanischen Touristengruppe. Nach Verführung der Reiseleiterin überzeugt er sie, dass eine Vernissage im Centre de Gravure interessanter sei als eine Besichtigung der UNO. Um 18.00 h platzen an die fünfzig japanische Touristen mitten in die Vernissage hinein. Unbeschwert lassen sie sich mit Einheimischen vor den Werken von Rosemarie Trockel fotografieren, prosten einander mit dem kredenzten Weißwein zu, lauschen aufmerksam den Erläuterungen der Reiseleiterin und verschwinden in ihren Bus. Der Veranstalter wollte Gianni Motti die Vernissage "animieren" lassen, der Künstler gestaltet sie zur Touristenattraktion um. Am 20. März 1998 erscheinen in Paris Mitglieder der Raël-Sekte auf einer Vernissage in der Galerie Jousse/Seguin. Wie es ihre Angewohnheit ist, schauen die Raëlianer ihrem jeweiligen Gegenüber starr in die Augen und beginnen von Gott zu sprechen, einem Außerirdischen, der uns alle durch Klonung erschaffen habe. Die "zufällige Begegnung" zwischen Gianni Motti und einer Touristengruppe oder Vertretern von Außerirdischen könnte als eine reine Zufälligkeit des Augenblicks erscheinen. Bei genauerem Hinsehen erhellen solche Begegnungen jedoch auf frappierende Weise das Vorgehen des Künstlers.

Gleich einem Touristen geht Gianni Motti spazieren. Wie viele heutige Künstler begibt er sich nicht mehr auf Forschungsreise wie ein gramzerfurchter Fitzcarraldo, bereit, sich mit allem zu prügeln, was ihm in die Quere kommt. Nein, er begibt sich gleitend ins Innere des Spektakels. Als Umberto Eco sich (vor bald zehn Jahren) die Frage stellte, welcher Fernsehserienheld in der Gunst des Volkes am höchsten stünde, setzte er ganz oben auf die Liste Inspektor Columbo (gleichauf allerdings mit Kommissar Derrick).[6] Gälte es ein Vorbild zu finden, das den Künstlern von heute gemeinsam ist, kein Zweifel, dass auch dabei der Inspektor die Wahl gewänne. Sicher, er ist nicht so begabt wie Superman. Er fliegt nicht mit Lichtgeschwindigkeit, und ein Supergehör wurde ihm ebensowenig zuteil wie der Röntgenblick. Wie Gianni Motti und seinesgleichen geht Columbo spazieren, schärft seine Neugier im Zuge des Gesprächs, kleidet sich in einem Supermarkt ein, trinkt gerne mal einen. Wie alle Welt. "Am Ende kommt alles heraus" – so der Titel einer seiner zahlreichen Untersuchungen – könnte sein Credo sein. Tatsächlich vollbringt der Inspektor zur Überführung des Täters keinerlei Heldentaten. Denn der gesteht letztlich immer, knickt ein unter dem Gewicht der Fangfragen. Wie Columbo, wie ein beliebiger Tourist, verlassen sich heutige Künstler ebensosehr auf ihren Riecher wie auf die Fügung der Umstände. Wie die neuen Piraten schreiten sie nicht mehr frontal zur Tat, mit dem Strumpf über dem Kopf, hysterischer Stimme und gut geölter Waffe. Vielmehr entwickeln sie Strategien der Infiltration, spannen Parallelnetze auf und verdrehen die Regeln der Sichtbarkeit.

Genauso vielsagend ist Gianni Mottis Begegnung mit Vertretern von Außerirdischen. Das Bild vom hysterischen kleinen grünen Männchen, das frenetisch die Laserpistole schwingt und alles plattmacht, was ihm unterkommt, ist überholt. Seit einigen Jahrzehnten schon sieht der Außerirdische dem Menschen zum Verwechseln ähnlich. Entweder wurde der Mensch anhand des Modells eines Außerirdischen geklont, oder der Außerirdische hat das Aussehen des Menschen angenommen. Letzteres ist eine faszinierende Option: sie erhellt eine ganze Richtung der aktuellen Kunst. Nur wenige winzige Indizien verraten den Außerirdischen (bei den niederen Chargen ein etwas steifer kleiner Finger zum Beispiel). Sobald man ihn identifiziert, kehrt er in seinen *Alien*-Status zurück. Doch wenn er aus unserem Alltag verschwindet, hat er dann auch unsere Realität verlassen? Kann er sich wirklich in ein *Außerhalb* der Realität verflüchtigen?

MULTIVERSE, VIDEOSPIELE UND QUANTENPHYSIK

Außerirdische erfüllen eine genau bestimmte Funktion: Neben der Tatsache, dass sie uns vor dem Fernseher unterhalten, helfen sie uns dabei, einen komplexeren Wirklichkeitsbegriff auszubilden als jenen, den der normale Menschenverstand uns aufzuerlegen versucht. Wenn unsere Welt uns realer erscheint als eine andere, so entfließt dieser Eindruck keiner Erfahrung (denn jede Welt erscheint ihren Bewohnern als die einzige Wirklichkeit), sondern einer philosophischen Auffassung von der Welt, die sich im Sensus Communis durchgesetzt hat.[7]

Ein weiterer Akteur von Belang ist in der Konstruktion eines umfassenderen Wirklichkeitsbegriffs zum Tragen gekommen: Videospiele. Seit deren Aufkommen verfügt jeder Spieler über mehrere Leben. Außerdem erreicht er kein besseres Leben durch strenge Moral oder gewissenhaft eingehaltene Riten, sondern durch die Geschicklichkeit, mit der er sich in dem Universum, das er sich aussucht, bewegt.

Dank der Astronomie ist der Wirklichkeitsbegriff mit Riesenschritten weitergediehen (oder, besser gesagt, komplexer geworden). Der erste Exoplanet wurde vor noch keinem Jahrzehnt beobachtet, und heute entdeckt man nahezu alle Tage einen. Eine solche Entwicklung führt bezüglich der berühmten Hypothese eines Lebens außerhalb des Sonnensystems zu einer völligen Kehrtwende. Angesichts der Anzahl derzeit beobachteter Exoplaneten müssen die Wissenschaftler einräumen, dass die Hypothese des Vorkommens von Leben in der Exosphäre wahrscheinlicher ist als die Hypothese eines ausschließlich irdischen Lebens.

Vielleicht ist es die Quantenphysik, die dem Wirklichkeitsverständnis die neuesten Perspektiven eröffnet. Der Professor für Quantenphysik David Deutsch hat in seinen Untersuchungen nachgewiesen, dass es zwar mehrere Universen geben kann, aber nur eine Realität. In seinem in diesem Buch abgedruckten Text erläutert Deutsch, dass man sich die Realität nicht auf ein Universum, sondern auf ein Multiversum bezogen vorstellen muss: "Die Realität besteht aus einem Multiversum, einem gewaltigen Gebilde, das *im groben Maßstab* eine Struktur aufweist, die einer Vielzahl von Kopien des Universums der klassischen Physik gleicht, aber in einem hinlänglich feinen Maßstab ein einziges, einheitliches System ist."[8] Im Interview mit einem Journalisten von *Philosophy Now* gibt David Deutsch eine eingehendere Erläuterung seiner Überlegungen zu Paralleluniversen. Wir bringen hier einen längeren Text, der aber erhellt, wie sehr es auf das ankommt, was wir in den multiplen Sphären der Wirklichkeit nicht sehen oder wahrnehmen:

"Beginnen wir mit der mikroskopischen Welt, denn nur auf der mikroskopischen Ebene finden wir direkte Beweise für Paralleluniversen. Der erste Schritt des Arguments fußt auf der Beobachtung, dass das Verhalten von Partikeln im Einzelschlitz-Experiment Vorgänge aufzeigt, die wir zwar nicht sehen, aber aufgrund ihrer Interferenzwirkungen auf Teilbereiche, die wir sehen, erkennen können. In einem zweiten Schritt stellen wir fest, dass dieser ungesehene Teil der mikroskopischen Welt den Teilbereich, den wir sehen, an Komplexität weit übertrifft. Am deutlichsten veranschaulicht dies der Quantencomputer: Wir wissen, dass ein Quantencomputer moderater Größe Berechnungen von enormer Komplexität anstellen könnte, einer Komplexität, die weiter reicht als das gesamte sichtbare Universum mit allen für uns wahrnehmbaren Atomen, und dies, obwohl der Quantencomputer selbst nur aus ein paar Hundert Atomen besteht. Das heißt, es gibt in der Wirklichkeit sehr viel mehr, als für uns sichtbar ist. Was wir sehen können, ist ein winziger Teil der Realität, und der übrige betrifft uns meistens nicht. In diesen speziellen Experimenten jedoch betreffen uns nur einige wenige Teile davon, und sogar diese Teile sind weitaus komplizierter als die Gesamtheit dessen, was wir sehen. Als einziger Zwischenschritt bleibt noch festzustellen, dass die Quantenmechanik, so wie wir sie bereits haben, jene anderen Teile der Wirklichkeit, jene Teile, die wir nicht sehen, genauso beschreibt wie die Teile, die wir sehen. Sie beschreibt auch die Interaktion zwischen den beiden, und wenn wir die Struktur des ungesehenen Teils analysieren, erkennen wir, dass sie weitestgehend aus vielen Kopien des Teils besteht, den wir sehen. Es handelt sich also nicht um ein monolithisches zweites Universum, das sehr kompliziert wäre und nach ganz anderen Regeln funktionieren würde oder dergleichen. Der ungesehene Teil verhält sich ganz ähnlich wie der gesehene Teil, nur dass es sehr viele Kopien davon gibt.

"Vergleichbares ergibt sich aus der Entdeckung anderer Planeten oder Galaxien. Früher kannten wir nur die Milchstraße, dann aber stellten wir nicht nur fest, dass es im Weltall eine riesige Anzahl von Sternen gibt – weitaus mehr als in der Milchstraße –, sondern auch mehr Galaxien im Weltall als Sterne in der Milchstraße. Ferner haben wir herausgefunden, dass die meisten Sterne außerhalb der Milchstraße ihrerseits in kleinen Milchstraßen organisiert sind. Und genauso verhält es sich mit dem Paralleluniversum. Das ist natürlich nur eine Analogie, aber eine recht gute; ganz so wie Sterne und Galaxien sind die ungesehenen Teile der Wirklichkeit in Gruppen organisiert, die dem sichtbaren Teil ähneln. Innerhalb einer solchen Gruppe, die wir als ein Paralleluniversum bezeichnen, können alle Partikel untereinander interagieren, was sie wiederum mit Partikeln aus anderen Universen kaum tun. Sie interagieren auf weitgehend gleiche Weise wie diejenigen, die in unserem sichtbaren Universum untereinander interagieren. Aus diesem Grund können wir von Universen sprechen. Parallel nennen wir sie deswegen, weil zwischen diesen Universen kaum Interaktionen vorkommen, so wie parallele Linien einander nicht kreuzen. Dieser Vergleich gilt jedoch nur näherungsweise, da im Zuge von Interferenzphänomenen ja leichte Interaktionen auftreten. Damit haben wir die Argumentationskette, die vom Parallelismus, der übrigens auf der mikroskopischen Ebene weitaus weniger umstritten ist als auf der makroskopischen Ebene, geradewegs zu Paralleluniversen führt. Philosophisch gesprochen, möchte ich hinzufügen, dass es einfach keinen Sinn ergibt, wenn wir davon ausgehen, dass es parallele Kopien aller Partikel gibt, die an mikroskopischen Interaktionen beteiligt sind, nicht aber parallele Kopien der makroskopischen. Das ist so, als sagte man, jemand verdoppele die Anzahl der Pennies auf einem Bankkonto, ohne die Anzahl an Pfund zu verdoppeln."[9]

Was wir sehen, stellt also laut Deutsch nur einen winzigen Teil der Realität dar. Die Realität ist in dem, was wir sehen oder wahrnehmen, nicht zu Ende, und was uns entgeht, jener "Rest", jenes "Unsichtbare", bildet ein unbegrenztes Gebiet, in dem unendlich viele Zusammenschlüsse stattfinden, die sich – den Erkenntnissen der Quantenphysiker zufolge – auf die gleiche Weise organisieren wie die sichtbare Welt. In diesem Sinne sind sie *Kopien* der sichtbaren Welt – daher stammt auch die möglicherweise absurd erscheinende Behauptung, es existiere in jedem Universum eine Kopie seiner selbst, aber die Gesamtheit der Kopien bilde nur eine einzige Realität.

Es ist interessant zu beobachten, auf welche Weise die Begriffe von Realität und Unsichtbarkeit sich in der Kunst entwickelt haben und in welchem Grad sie sich heute den neueren Beschäftigungen der Physiker annähern. "Das Unsichtbare sehen", die Forderung vieler Künstler in der ersten Hälfte des 20. Jahrhunderts, zielte auf die Erkundung der Gebiete, die sich der sichtbaren Welt entzogen. Diese Gebiete wurden als "jenseits des Wirklichen" betrachtet, als *terra incognita*, die die Künstler gleich Erforschern des Unbewussten erschließen würden. In der Kunst wie anderswo auch zogen die Helden zur Eroberung neuer Gegenden aus, als deren Erlöser zurückzukehren sie sich schuldig waren: Dank ihrer gewann die Realität neue Räume, konnte sich ausdehnen und über-leben. Der Außerirdische besaß unschlagbare Waffen, um den Planeten Erde zu erobern, Superman bezwang die Schwerkraft, um den Planeten Erde zu retten, und der Künstler verfügte über transzendentale Inspirationen, um die vielen verborgenen Gesichter des Planeten Erde zu entschleiern. Über der Realität, den Gesetzen, den physikalischen und psychischen Banalitäten schwebend, konnten alle drei dem "einfachen Sterblichen" einen präzisen Platz innerhalb der Realität zuweisen. "Das Unsichtbare sehen" hieß im besten Fall, jungfräuliche Gebiete auftun, neue Zonen, Plattformen, die man besetzen konnte. Es hieß aber vor allem, einen ganz bestimmten Punkt bezeichnen, der sich dadurch defi-nierte, was sich unserem Realitätsverständnis entzog und jenseits unserer gewöhnlichen Wahrnehmung zu liegen schien.

DAS REALE: WIE VIELE SCHICHTEN?

Ganz anders stellt sich die Kunst heute dar – hat sie doch, nicht weiter überraschend, die gleiche Entwicklung genommen wie die Helden, die Außerirdischen und die Quanten-physik. Man erinnert sich an Stalins berühmte Frage: "Der Papst: Wie viele Divisionen?" Entsprechend könnte man sich heute fragen: "Die Realität: Wie viele Schichten?" Eine Frage, die weitere Fragen nach sich zieht: Wie weit kann man die Realität dehnen, bis sie zerreißt? Wie viele zusätzliche Schichten kann man der Realität aufpfropfen, bevor sie einstürzt?" Heute wirken solche Fragen ebenso absurd wie die einst von Stalin gestellte. In der Tat, je weiter das Jahrhundert voranschritt, als desto komplexer erwies sich das Reale. Und je vielfältigere Anstrengungen zu seiner Analyse unternommen wurden, desto mehr offenbarte es eine unglaubliche Elastizität, einen unzerreißbaren Körper, der beliebig dehnbar und faltbar ist. Dass es keinen Fixpunkt im Universum gebe, behauptete bereits Einstein. Angesichts dieser schrecklichen Feststellung musste man sich organi-sieren. Oblag die heikle Aufgabe, die genauen Grenzen zu zeichnen, wo der Mensch seinen Ort finden könne, einst den Übermenschen aller Spielarten, so hat die Lage sich seit einigen Jahrzehnten radikal verändert. Heutige Helden bekommen Schnupfen, schlagen sich mit Haarschuppen herum, achten auf ihr Gewicht, haben Prostataleiden, wandern ins

Gefängnis und/oder sterben an Krebs. So ungefähr wie alle Welt. Nur noch ein paar utopische Romantiker glauben an so etwas wie eine *Mission Impossible*. Für gewöhnlich rekrutieren sie sich aus dem Sportmilieu (am längsten laufen oder am schnellsten fahren), dem Parasportmilieu (Weltumrundung im Fesselballon oder Überquerung des Atlantiks) oder dem des Kinos (Verkörperung Jesu oder seiner Avatare, Erlösungsspezialisten aller Sorten wie Napoleon, Gandhi, Kennedy oder Jim Morrison). Aber es gelingt ihnen nicht lange, den Leuten etwas vorzumachen. Beim Koksschnüffeln erwischt, bei der Steuer-hinterziehung, beim Kratzen der Unterleibsregion oder bei der Lektüre des IKEA-Katalogs aufgeflogen, werden sie früher oder später von ihrer conditio humana verraten.

Damit muss man sich abfinden: Es wird immer schwieriger, als Bevollmächtigter zu leben. An Vergöttlichungsanwärtern herrscht zwar kein Mangel, aber keiner hält länger als eine Saison durch. Angesichts dieser Lücke verwischen sich die Grenzen der Realität so unerbittlich, wie die Wüste vorrückt. Daher die große Angst der Philosophen heute: Die Gegenwart gleitet auf der Oberfläche der Zeit und macht eine Erfassung einer durch klar umgrenzte Zeitmarken bestimmten Realität unmöglich. Eingetaucht in eine Weltzeit, erleben wir eine Kompression von Vergangenheit, Gegenwart und Zukunft und sind völlig in die Unmittelbarkeit, die Instantaneität verstrickt. Unter der Herrschaft der "Realzeit" kann die Gegenwart nur *vergehen*[10] in einer Bewegung durchlaufenden Transits, stän-digen Gleitens. Manche Philosophen wie Virilio zum Beispiel beunruhigen sich über eine solche durch die Sprengung der überlieferten Zeitorientierungen gekennzeichnete Situa-tion, in der der Mensch den permanenten Transfer nicht mehr bremsen kann (und will) und alle Hoffnung verliert, zu Handlungsweisen zurückzufinden, mit denen er seine Ver-fasstheit des In-der-Welt-Seins begründen könnte. Wie lässt sich in einem der Grenzen entledigten Universum leben, wenn doch gerade die Suche nach solchen Grenzen einen für unser Gleichgewicht konstitutiven Akt ausmacht? Dieses Paradox steht bei Humani-sten aller Richtungen im Kern der Überlegungen.

Im Allgemeinen als ein Hinderns betrachtet, das es zu überwinden, ein Übel, das es auszumerzen gelte, stellt dieses *Entgleiten* der Welt die Kunst vor eine fantastische Herausforderung. Anstatt sich von ihm zu distanzieren, schließt die aktuelle Kunst sich ihm an und übernimmt dieselbe Dynamik. Die heutigen Künstler überlassen das Bestreben, neue Plattformen zu errichten, der Vergangenheit, haben sich verabschiedet vom Glauben an die Tauglichkeit der Zwischenräume, der sich durch die Kunst der neunziger Jahre zieht, und engagieren sich vielmehr in einer Tätigkeit, die langwierig, ja gefährlich erscheinen mag. "Ein von vorneherein verlorener Kampf", werden ihre Eltern kopfschüttelnd klagen. Man wird ihnen Ben's berühmte Formel entgegenhalten: "Kunst ist ein schmutziges Geschäft, aber irgendwer muss es ja machen." Die Künstler treiben diese Neigung, sich gehen zu lassen, dem Vorrücken der Wüste nicht länger zu widerstehen, von der anbrandenden Welle mitgespült zu werden, die alle Spuren, alle Grenzen verwischt, zum Äußersten. Nicht dass sie beschlossen hätten, den Fernseher auszuschalten, das Rauchen aufzugeben und sich auf die *wahren* Werte unserer Gesellschaft zu konzentrieren. Nein, sie schauen Bier trinkend *Big Brother*, schlafen bis in die Puppen und lesen Boulevardzeitungen. Doch statt an diesem Sachverhalt zu leiden und sich an jedem Ersten des Jahres aufzulehnen mit dem Vorsatz "dieses Jahr ändere ich mich", tauchen sie ein ins Innere des Entgleitens, so wie Parasiten die Funktionsweise ihres Wirtes annehmen. Die Arbeit von Peter Fischli / David Weiss bildet in dieser Hinsicht ein Musterbeispiel.

Fortsetzung in der nächsten Episode

Episode 16
WARTEN AUF SONNTAG

SOLL ICH DIE BETTWÄSCHE WECHSELN?

1978 besuchen Peter Fischli / David Weiss ein Möbelkaufhaus in einem Zürcher Außenbezirk. Lange flanieren sie umher, ehe sie – sprachlos – vor einem marokkanischen Puff stehenbleiben. Ein Jahr später beginnen sie eine künstlerische Zusammenarbeit, deren ungemeiner Reichtum und Erfindersinn 25 Jahre später ermessbar wird.

Die Arbeit von Peter Fischli / David Weiss zu analysieren, kann ein Schwindelgefühl vergleichbar den dynamischen Verkettungen und Bewegungen ihres berühmten Films *Der Lauf der Dinge* (1987) hervorrufen: Jede Sache ist Ursache der folgenden, jedes Objekt in eine Kettenreaktion eingebunden, und diese uferlose Abfolge scheint kein Ende zu finden, sich auf kein bestimmtes oder auch nur identifizierbares Konzept festzulegen.

Worin besteht die kausale Beziehung zwischen einer Scheibe Mortadella, einem Abflussrohr, einem Schneemann, einem Blumenkohl, einer Betonlandschaft, einem auf einer Möhre balancierenden Gewürzgürkchen, einem Brot, einer Lokomotive, der Rollbahn eines Flughafens, bunten Blumen, einem Polyurethan-Eimer, den ägyptischen Pyramiden?

Bereits 1984[11] stellen Peter Fischli / David Weiss ein Verzeichnis vordringlich zu lösender Fragen auf: *Ist nicht alles eine Frage der Zeit? Soll ich die Bettwäsche wechseln? Gibt es ein Leben im Weltraum? Werde ich geliebt? Bis wohin kann man gehen? Kann man alles falsch machen? Noch ein Gläschen?"*

Wo sind die Antworten? Peter Fischli lächelt und spricht von einer "Schizophrenie der Empfindungen". Man könnte hinzufügen: einem Entgleiten der Wahrnehmungen. Denn wer betrachtet ihre Bilder wirklich, beispielsweise die absichtsvoll banalen *Bilder, Ansichten* (1991)? Sie zeigen, was jeder kennt, was kollektiv in das visuelle Gedächtnis eingeschrieben ist. Ein Sehen und Zeigen dessen, was der Sensus Communis von einer beruhigenden Illustration, einem schönen Bild erwartet, etwas, das sofort identifizierbar ist und dessen Deutungsschlüssel einhellig geteilt werden.[12] Archetypische Bilder. Pyramiden, Flughäfen, Sonnenuntergänge am Strand, Eiffelturm, gerade geborenes Kätzchen, sonnenüberflutete rote Äpfel, Matterhorn, Grand Canyon. Bilder, die man tausend Mal auf allen Postkarten der Welt gesehen hat und anlässlich derer selbst John Waters, der Fürst des schlechten Geschmacks, sich fragte, wer als erster Gutes über *Flughäfen* [13] gesagt habe, um dann doch zu gestehen, dass er in diesen Klischees einen neuen Typus von Schönheit sehe, einen neuen Typus von Kunstwerk, über das es rein gar nichts zu sagen gebe. Noch einmal das Matterhorn oder einen Sonnenuntergang zu sehen, ist nicht unangenehm. Ohnedies schaut man diese Bilder, die man seit jeher vor Augen hat, nicht mehr wirklich an. Man *gleitet* über sie hinweg, um an etwas anderes zu denken. An die Ferien letztes Jahr, in diesem zauberhaften Chalet. An die Fernsehserie, die man im Familienkreis gesehen hat.

DIE ZEIT AUSFÜLLEN. LOB DER LANGSAMKEIT UND ÄSTHETIK DES GLEITENS

Diese Fotografien sind nicht *ready made*. Peter Fischli / David Weiss haben sich nicht damit begnügt, aus einer umfangreichen Datenbank die Bilder zu fischen, die ihnen als die bezeichnendsten vorkamen. Reisen, Flanieren, Warten auf den günstigsten Augenblick und der Wunsch, Aufnahmen zu schießen, die den schönsten Postkarten in nichts nachstehen, sind weit gewichtigere Beweggründe. Diese Absicht, die durch das Ready Made erworbene Kraft und Aura auf den Prüfstand zu stellen, findet sich auch in einer so völlig andersartigen Arbeit wie *Der Tisch* (1992) wieder. Auf einem riesigen Holztablett sind kunterbunt zusammengewürfelte Dinge zu sehen, vom Reinigungsmittel über Farbdosen, Backsteine, Schokolade, Hocker, Pinzette, Kanister, eine Coladose u.a.m. bis zum Hunde-kuchen. Es könnte sich um eine Ansammlung von Objekten im Atelier des Künstlers handeln, nur mit dem Unterschied, dass alle auf der Platte ausgestellten Gegenstände akribisch aus Polyurethan gefertigt sind, einem Werkstoff, den die Künstler von Anfang an benutzten. Andere Arbeiten, wie der 1987 entstandene marokkanische Puff, wurden aus schwarzem Gummi hergestellt. Ein Ready Made hingegen wird nicht hergestellt, es taucht plötzlich auf, transfiguriert von einem Zustand in einen anderen. Wie Boris Groys[14] in einem spannenden Aufsatz darlegt, hat das Kunstwerk im Lauf des vergangenen Jahr-hunderts Lichtgeschwindigkeit erreicht, weil seine Produktion sich so schnell wie ein Gedanke vollzieht und lediglich von einem Entschluss abhängt. Peter Fischli / David Weiss legen demgegenüber ein großangelegtes Entschleunigungsunternehmen vor. Die von ihnen erstellten Arbeiten unterscheiden sich in nichts von unseren alltäglichen Gebrauchs-gegenständen. Man macht sich gefasst auf Fabrikprodukte, Indizien unseres maschinellen

Zeitalters. Stattdessen trifft man auf "handgemachte" Objekte, die in einer der handwerklichen Fertigungsweise eigenen Langsamkeit entstanden sind. Peter Fischli / David Weiss kommt es nun nicht darauf an, die Tugenden des Handwerkers zu preisen. Die Langsamkeit ist mit der Zeit verbunden, und für sie ist das stetige Arbeiten "nützlich verschwendete Zeit". Die Langsamkeit kann auch die des Flanierens, des Spaziergangs sein. Sie ist daher verknüpft mit der existenziellen Frage: Wie die Zeit erfolgreich ausfüllen? Was tun an einem Sonntagnachmittag? Was sieht man beim Flanieren? Meistens nichts Besonderes. Wir spazieren in einer Umgebung, die unsere Wachträumerei speist. In dieses "Nichts Besondere" haben Peter Fischli / David Weiss mit einem Werk eingegriffen, das auf zwölf Monitoren über 80 Stunden lang Videos zeigt (XLVI. Biennale in Venedig, 1995). Gefilmt haben die Künstler die Wegstrecke zwischen ihrer Wohnung und dem Atelier, einen Ausflug in die Alpen, ein Indoor-Motocross-Rennen, die Herstellung von Käse. In Zürich streifen sie durch die Stadt und beobachten die Leute beim Autowaschen, beim Kaufen eines Würstchens am Stand. Dazu gibt es keinen Kommentar. Keinerlei Absicht, sich von einer neutralen TV-Ästhetik abzuheben. Das Ganze erinnert stark an die "No-Comment"-Sequenzen auf Euronews. Nur dass nichts passiert. Keiner schießt in die Menge. Die Künstler filmen schlicht und einfach das, was sie im Augenblick interessiert. Wenn man die Zeit ausfüllt, lauert man auf das kleinste Ereignis. Man stellt eine Rangordnung der interessanten Dinge auf. Man beschließt, einer Szene, und sei sie noch so belanglos, nachzugehen, zu Ungunsten einer anderen. Man wartet darauf, dass "etwas passiert", und sowohl im Leben als auch in den Videos von Peter Fischli / David Weiss passiert selten etwas. Und dieses Warten auf das Wesentliche macht oftmals das Wesentliche am Warten aus. Man wartet ungeduldig auf Sonntag. Sonntags langweilt man sich bekanntlich, und letzten Endes ist es gerade das Warten, das sich als der spannendste Moment entpuppt.

Peter Fischli / David Weiss macht das Flanieren Spaß. Ein Jahr lang haben sie Blumen, Pilze und Gemüsegärten fotografiert, wobei sie eine Anfängertechnik benutzten: die Doppelbelichtung. Das Ergebnis ist verwirrend. "Wie schön!" ruft man, doch im selben Moment meldet sich der kritische Verstand, der Wert darauf legt, sich nicht beeindrucken zu lassen. Die doppelte Belichtung der Naturschönheiten ruft zwiespältige Gefühle hervor und erinnert an die oben erwähnte "Ästhetik der Schizophrenie". In einer erstmals 1999 gezeigten Installation [15] projizieren Peter Fischli / David Weiss diese Bilder an die Raum- wände. Dank der Überblendungstechnik überschneidet sich jedes Dia – bereits Ergebnis einer Doppelbelichtung – mit dem nachfolgenden, das Ganze gespeist von einem ununter- brochen kreisenden Karussell. Diese Vierfachbelichtung ist Schwindel erregend. In Anbe- tracht des völligen Fehlens von Fixpunkten kann das Auge nur über die Bilder gleiten. Das Sehen gerät ins Wanken, berauscht von dieser Illusion fortwährender Bewegung, an die uns das Kino gewöhnt hat. Es bewegt sich nicht mehr im Bereich der Beobachtung, sondern des *Verlaufs*. Doch im Unterschied zum Kino erleben wir einen Verlauf ohne Ziel, ohne Anfang noch Ende, einen Verlauf, der nur Durchgang, Vergehen ist. Und wie ihre Bilder, die einander überlagernd vorbeiziehen, so gehen auch die Künstler nur durch.

Im Gegensatz zu den Vertretern der Land Art, die aus ihren Ateliers hinauszogen, um *on the road* die gigantischen Weiten Amerikas nach einem belehnbaren Ort abzusuchen, belehnen die Künstler von heute überhaupt nichts mehr. Sie brechen nicht zur Forschungs- reise auf, sie gehen spazieren. Sie positionieren sich nicht mehr gegenüber der Land- schaft, sie gleiten in sie hinein. Das Spazierengehen birgt eine wirksame und heilsame Eigenschaft: es füllt die Zeit aus. Und es ermöglicht es den Künstlern, der fortwährenden Transitbewegung, die unsere "Realzeit" konstituiert, nicht passiv zu unterliegen, sondern sich der durch die Instantaneität unserer Gegenwart auferlegten Geschwindigkeit anzu- passen und eine regelrechte *Ästhetik des Gleitens* auszuarbeiten.

Aus dem Französischen von Stefan Barmann, Köln

1   Wie aus dem Textverlauf schnell hervorgeht, bietet sich für den französi-
    schen Begriff der *furtivité* keine deutsche Entsprechung an, die der Band-
    breite und Abgrenzung seiner Bedeutung gerecht wird. Ich habe mich
    deshalb für den unterdessen einschlägig bekannten englischen Ausdruck
    stealth entschieden, der das Verkappte, Nicht-Ortbare, Flüchtige, Unter-
    schwellige mit einschließt. A.d.Ü.

2   Marc-Olivier Wahler, *Transfert. Art dans l'espace urbain*, S. 29. Edition
    Transfert, Bienne 2000. Das Konzept der *furtivité* (Stealth, Flüchtigkeit,
    Verkapptheit) hat Alexandre Szames in seinem Aufsatz "Esthétique de la
    furtivité" entwickelt, in: *5, 6, 7, 8, 9 CAN*, édition CAN, Neuchâtel 2000,
    S. 42. (Dieser 1998-1999 geschriebene Text greift einige Thesen wieder
    auf, die der Verfasser bereits in seinem Text "Esthétique de la furtivité"
    dargelegt hat, in: *Crash*, n°2, März/April 1998.)

3   Wallace Matthews, Journalist bei der *New York Post*. Zitiert von Fred
    Hirzel (*Le Temps*, Rubrik Sport, Donnerstag, 14. März 2002) in einem
    Kommentar darüber, dass Mike Tyson am 13. März grünes Licht für
    die Rückkehr in den Ringe bekommen hatte. Der Ausdruck
    "Tier der Apokalypse" ist ihm entlehnt.

4   "She is an avid golfer, helps steer FOCA and creates gourmet meals.
    She is married to Mike Tyson and has both ears. Sarah has been a docent
    at SITE Santa Fe for five years."
    http://www.sitesantafe.org/general/contacts.html

5   Gilles Lipovetsky, *L'ère du vide*, Gallimard, 1983, S. 107. (dt. Ausgabe:
    Narziss oder die Leere. Sechs Kapitel über die unaufhörliche Gegenwart,
    Frankfurt a. M. 1995.)

6   Umberto Eco, "Conclusion 1993", in *De Superman au surhomme*, Grasset,
    Paris 1993, S. 210. Zitiert von Marc-Olivier Wahler in: *Transfert. Art dans
    l'espace urbain*, S. 29. Edition Transfert, Bienne 2000.

7   Lies hierzu die auf Seite 50-58 abgedruckte Korrespondenz zwischen
    David Deutsch und Seth Loyd, "Are parallel universes equally real? Brain
    tennis: David Deutsch vs Seth Loyd", Erstveröffentlichung
    am 9. Julyi 1997 auf http://hotwired.lycos.com/synapse.

8   Ebenda, Seite 50-58.

9   Filiz Peach, "Gespräch mit David Deutsch", in: *Philosophy Now*,
    Nr. 30, Dezember 2000.

10 "Diese Welt, so wie wir sehen, ist im Vergehen begriffen", Paulus von
    Tarsus, zitiert nach Paul Virilio, *Esthétique de la disparition*, éd. Galilée,
    Paris 1989, S. 9. (dt. Ausgabe: *Ästhetik des Verschwindens*, Berlin 1986)

11 *Fragentopf*. Die Fragen stehen auf dem Boden eines Polyurethan-
    Gefäßes.

12 "Unerfindlich, ob sie Fotos machen, um sich an die Reise zu erinnern,
    oder die Reise unternehmen, um Aufnahmen zu machen." (Christophe
    Domino, "Petite encyclopédie portative", in: *Peter Fischli/David Weiss*,
    Musée national d'art moderne, éd. Centre Georges Pompidou, Paris 1992.

13 John Waters, "Airports", in: *Vogue*, New York 1990.

14 Boris Groys, "The Speed of Art", in *Peter Fischli/David Weiss. XLVI
    Biennale di Venezia*, éd. OFC, Bern 1995.

15 Musée d'art moderne de la Ville de Paris.

EXTRA

Never get out of the boat. Absolutely goddamn right.
Unless you were going all the way.

Captain Willard, Apocalypse Now

Résumé des épisodes précédents

Mike Tyson ne constitue pas seulement un phénomène extraordinaire dans l'histoire de la boxe, il offre également une clé de lecture à un pan entier de l'art d'aujourd'hui. La puissance et surtout la rapidité de ses coups forcent le téléspectateur à s'interroger sur les notions de *furtivité* et de *photogénie* perceptibles dans l'image de ses combats. Une de mes cassettes vidéo préférées retrace *Les meilleurs K.O. de Mike Tyson*. Ce qui me frappe chaque fois que je vois le malheureux challenger s'écrouler, c'est que le coup asséné par Tyson est invisible. Il est si rapide qu'il devient furtif[1], si brutal qu'il devient photogénique. Je passe la scène au ralenti, je vois l'amorce de l'attaque puis – sans transition – le poing d'Iron Mike écrasé sur la figure de l'adversaire qui tombe comme un poids mort. Ni le spectateur, ni (de manière évidente) l'adversaire n'a vu le coup dans son intégralité (son temps, sa trajectoire). S'il est invisible, de quelle manière s'inscrit-il dans notre réalité, et comment peut-il devenir aussi spectaculaire ? La fascination qu'exerce Tyson sur le commun des mortels tient à cette double présence paradoxale des notions de furtivité et de photogénie. Il se trouve que depuis quelques années ces deux notions sont devenues un concept-clé éclairant les codes de représentation et les constructions de réalités nouvelles mis en œuvre par nombre d'artistes actuels.

Épisode 14
BOXE, FURTIVITÉ, APOCALYPSE,
VIOL ET ART CONTEMPORAIN

ENTRE LE FURTIF ET LE PHOTOGÉNIQUE

On ne soulignera jamais assez que la notion de furtivité, certes initiée et régentée par les militaires, a effectivement traversé le monde de l'art comme une onde de choc. La furtivité n'a rien à voir avec le camouflage. Le but du camouflage est de dissimuler. Un objet camouflé adopte formes et couleurs lui permettant non pas d'être invisible, mais de passer inaperçu. Il se travestit, se cache. On est en présence d'une technique de chasse ancestrale, d'une pratique guerrière centenaire. Devenu un standard définitivement fashion (même si certaines armées recourent encore à ce procédé séculaire car bon marché), le camouflage incarne aux yeux des guerriers d'aujourd'hui une méthode de couard. Laissons aux soldats de bas-étages leur jeu "tu-te-caches-dans-une-grotte-et-je-te-largue-un-maximum-de-bombes". Dans un combat de rue par exemple, celui qui a le malheur de se cacher est un lâche, une mauviette, une lavette.

Tout autre se révèle l'objet furtif. Sa qualité principale est de briser toute signature optique ; il dévie, fractionne ou absorbe les signaux. Il mute, feint. Il ne se dissimule pas : il esquive les techniques de reconnaissance par signal. Mais l'objet furtif peut aussi demeurer parfaitement visible à l'œil nu. La furtivité (défaut de visible) peut – en un éclair – se transformer en son exacte opposé : le photogénique (excès de visible). Un bombardier furtif, par exemple, se dérobe à la vue des radars. Pour ces instruments de mesure, il est invisible, absent. Or l'œil humain n'éprouve aucune peine à le distinguer. Et une fois visible, il devient non seulement vulnérable, mais surtout hyper spectaculaire. Il est alors photogénique. Invisible *et* hyper spectaculaire, furtif *et* photogénique, un tel objet offre un paradoxe absolument stupéfiant qui n'a pas échappé à l'attention des artistes.

BÊTE DE L'APOCALYPSE

En ce sens, Mike Tyson est un cas exemplaire. S'il est la créature capable d'assommer son adversaire par un coup invisible (qui semble venir de nulle part pour finir violemment sa course sur la figure de son adversaire), il incarne également un modèle basé sur une hyper-spectacularité de l'événement. Vus d'un téléviseur, ses coups surgissent du néant. Apparemment, de cette marge invisible de l'intervalle qui lie 24 images par seconde et qui, *in exten*so, forme le film notre réalité.

Le paradoxe de l'objet furtif demeure entier chez Tyson. Ses coups échappent à la vigilance du signal cathodique (visuellement, ils n'existent pas). Mais dans le même temps, ce qui est donné à voir ressort de l'hyper spectaculaire et témoigne d'un excès du visible. Un homme invulnérable avec son adversaire à terre. L'impact de cette image certes saisissante est sur-multipliée par la personnalité du boxeur, un champion accusé de viol, renonçant à tout contrôle de soi, écrasant tout sur son passage, que ce soit l'automobiliste qui ne lui cède pas la priorité, Miss Black America qui tarde à se mettre à genou, l'arbitre qui tente d'arrêter le massacre ou, plus récemment, le garde du corps de son futur adversaire esquissant un geste paraissant suspect. Et s'il n'écrase pas son adversaire, Mike Tyson le mord sauvagement, dans une action qui s'apparente au cannibalisme autant qu'à une technique de combat.

Mike Tyson est l'incarnation contemporaine de la bête de l'apocalypse. "[Il] est sans doute celui que tout le monde dit. Le mauvais. L'animal. Le cinglé. Mais au moins, contrairement à ceux qui le qualifient ainsi, il n'est pas un hypocrite. Il est exactement celui que l'on veut qu'il soit (…). Il est allé en prison pour viol. Il a frappé des adversaires à terre. Il a volontairement cherché à casser le bras d'un autre. (…) Depuis dix ans, il a été moins boxeur que personnage d'épouvante. Il est une catastrophe en puissance, un naufrage total et programmé, pour lequel vous êtes tous prêts à payer, pour être là quand il se produira, pour vous faire peur le jour où cela arrivera. C'est pourquoi il est un must pour la télévision. [Ses combats] passionnent l'opinion parce qu'il s'agit d'un film d'horreur avec le meilleur acteur possible dans cet emploi."[2]

LE VIOLEUR VIOLÉ

Si un tel comportement assure au boxeur une gloire planétaire et une fortune colossale, Mike Tyson sait pourtant qu'il aurait tout intérêt à se comporter plus subtilement. Cela lui éviterait la prison, la condamnation générale des médias et la mise au ban de la communauté de la boxe. Quelque part, il aimerait bien être aimé et reconnu uniquement pour ses qualités pugilistiques. Mais au fond de lui-même, il y a toujours cette voix qui le pousse à ne pas écouter les sirènes du socialement correct et à agir en conformité avec son image d'exterminateur diabolique. Et il lutte. Il lutte aussi longtemps qu'il peut pour se conformer aux standards d'une société policée, où l'homme respecte la femme, l'automobiliste adresse un geste amical au conducteur d'en face, le sportif serre la main de son valeureux adversaire. Une société idéale définie par une chaleureuse solidarité, un respect sans distinction et un sourire permanent.

Pour s'y adapter, Iron Mike est prêt à tous les sacrifices. Il se gave d'antidépresseurs. Il épouse la charmante Sarah Tyson, que le Département de l'éducation de Santa Fe décrit comme une excellente étudiante en beaux-arts, experte en pastels, peinture à l'huile et gastronomie[3]. Il embrasse même l'Islam, passage obligé quand on est un boxeur noir et que l'on croupit plus de six mois en prison. Il lutte, mais à chaque fois qu'il s'approche de la reconnaissance sociale (– "Allez, Mike, c'est bon, on te pardonne ! Mike, souris au journaliste ! Mike, dis que tu aimes ce yoghourt. Mike, signe ici en bas à droite !"), une voix résonne et le pousse à saboter les efforts entrepris. (– "Non, Mike, ne te laisse pas ensorceler par cette tiédeur sociale, refuse cette image sournoise du "bon black" qui a réussi son intégration dans l'univers du blanc. Mike, tu n'es pas Colin Powell, tu es la terreur des rues, le cauchemar des dames, le Ben Laden de la boxe ! MIKE, ATTAQUE !")

Mike est piégé. Qu'il opte pour une ascension vers les cimes du socialement correct ou pour un plongeon dans le chaudron de l'apocalypse, l'issue se révèle toujours fatale. Quel que soit son choix, une moitié de son être viole l'autre. En constante effraction avec elle-même, son âme se déchire et se déchaîne contre ses adversaires, ses femmes ou tout autre être humain qui croise sa route. Du furtif au photogénique, Mike Tyson glisse sur la surface du réel sans pouvoir le fixer, l'immobiliser pour en prendre la mesure. Il tente de transpercer ce réel qui lui échappe en abattant son entourage. Mais comme dans ce jeu où l'on tape sur des marmottes qui disparaissent pour ressurgir par un autre trou, le réel refait toujours surface.

Plus Mike prend de l'âge, plus il s'éloigne de ce modèle moderniste où l'on pouvait aisément le considérer (ainsi que d'autre sportifs ou artistes) comme un chevalier invincible, doué d'une force venue d'une autre planète, tel un extra-terrestre ayant contre son gré adopté l'apparence d'un humain, mais bien décidé à montrer à la planète Terre qu'il n'est PAS un humain et qu'il nous détruira tous jusqu'au dernier. Mais ses pouvoirs ne peuvent rien contre l'effet de réel. L'adversaire finit par se relever pour finalement l'envoyer au tapis ou en prison. Toute la vie de Mike alterne entre ces deux états : le *sur-homme*, l'*alien* (figure qu'il incarnait véritablement à ses débuts, mais qui s'est inexorablement transformé en "histoire", voire en "légende") et le *sous-homme*, un être pathétique exploité de toute part, une ombre furtive en quête d'une âme. L'histoire de Mike Tyson pourrait se résumer en un titre de film : "Le fabuleux destin du violeur violé". Cette analogie au viol nous permet d'opérer un retour sur les concepts de furtivité et de photogénie développés plus haut. Car si le propre d'un objet doué d'absence et d'excès de visible est de briser sa signature optique et de déjouer les systèmes de reconnaissance, le but recherché en dernière instance est le viol d'un territoire, la pénétration d'une zone par tous les moyens, qu'ils soient softs, déviés, invisibles, déceptifs et furtifs ou frontaux, violents, spectaculaires et photogéniques.

Les artistes d'aujourd'hui articulent leur pratique sur des modèles inspirés de telles stratégies. Ils développent des tactiques d'infiltration, multiplient les réseaux et faussent les règles de visibilité. Ils ne se placent plus en héros romantiques affrontant le reste du monde, tels des John Wayne sur leurs chevaux blancs. Ils glissent à la surface du paysage. Conscients que le réel n'est plus un territoire à défricher, mais bien un supermarché climatisé, surchargé d'informations, un lieu de transit où le déplacement est impératif, ils règlent volontairement leur rythme de croisière sur celui de leur voisin de palier. Ils s'infiltrent dans la masse des pendulaires anesthésiés par la banalité de leurs gestes quotidiens. Ils adoptent un principe de mobilité constante et semblent confirmer cette "indifférence dont est affecté désormais le réel"[4]. Mais lorsqu'ils font mine de s'immobiliser, la réalité semble bouleversée. Un simple détail, d'ordinaire invisible, prend une dimension spectaculaire. Il devient photogénique. De nouveaux paradigmes émergent… Sans crier gare, les artistes sont entrés par effraction dans notre système interprétatif. A la fois démoniaques et médiatiques, ils opèrent à la vue de tous, mais dans la marge, dans un pli qui ne cesse de se déplier, dans un constant transit qui rend leurs actions à la fois invisibles et hyper spectaculaires, anonymes et scandaleuses.

Épisode 15
MISE EN GLISSE

LE TOURISTE ET L'EXTRATERRESTRE

Lorsqu'il est invité par des centres d'art ou galeries à "créer l'événement" le soir du vernissage, Gianni Motti se garde bien d'effectuer une quelconque performance personnelle. Il disparaît et laisse sa place aux acteurs de la réalité. Le 27 septembre 1997 à Genève, il détourne un car de touristes japonais. Après avoir séduit la guide, il la persuade qu'un vernissage au Centre de Gravure est plus intéressant qu'une visite de l'ONU. A 18 heures, une cinquantaine de touristes japonais débarque en plein milieu du vernissage. Hilares, ils se font photographier devant les œuvres de Trockel en compagnie d'autochtones, font "campei" avec le vin blanc offert, écoutent attentivement les explications de la guide et disparaissent dans leur bus. Le centre d'art voulait que Gianni Motti "anime" le vernissage, l'artiste l'a transformé en attraction touristique. Le 20 mars 1998 à Paris, les membres de la secte de Raël font leur apparition pendant un vernissage à la galerie Jousse/Seguin. Comme à leur habitude, les Raëliens fixent leur interlocuteur droit dans les yeux et évoquent Dieu, un extraterrestre qui nous a tous créés par clonage. La "rencontre fortuite" de Gianni Motti et d'un groupe de touristes ou de représentants d'extraterrestres peut sembler le fruit d'un pur hasard. A y regarder de plus près, de telles rencontres éclairent de manière frappante la démarche de l'artiste.

Tel un touriste, Gianni Motti se promène. Comme beaucoup d'artistes aujourd'hui, il ne part plus en expédition, tel un Fitzcarraldo tourmenté, prêt à en découdre avec tout ce qui peut lui barrer la route. Il se glisse à l'intérieur du spectacle. Se demandant (il y a bientôt 10 ans) quel héros de séries télévisées saurait conquérir la faveur populaire, Umberto Eco plaçait le lieutenant Columbo en tête de liste (à égalité tout de même avec l'inspecteur Derrick)[5]. S'il fallait trouver un modèle commun aux artistes d'aujourd'hui, nul doute que le lieutenant remporterait également les suffrages. Il n'est certes pas aussi doué que Superman. Il ne vole pas à la vitesse de la lumière et ne bénéfice ni d'une superouïe, ni d'une vue à rayon X. Columbo, comme Gianni Motti et ses pairs, se promène, aiguise sa curiosité au gré de la conversation, achète ses vêtements dans un supermarché, boit des verres. Comme tout le monde. "Tout finit par se savoir" – titre d'une de ses nombreuses "enquêtes" – pourrait être son credo. Le lieutenant n'accomplit en effet pas la moindre action héroïque pour débusquer le coupable. Ce dernier finit toujours par avouer, s'effondrant sous le poids des insinuations. Comme Columbo, comme n'importe quel touriste, les artistes d'aujourd'hui se fient autant à leur flair qu'au hasard des circonstances. Comme les nouveaux pirates, ils ne mènent plus d'actions frontales, le bas sur la tête, la voix menaçante, l'arme bien graissée. Ils développent des stratégies d'infiltration, élaborent des réseaux parallèles et faussent les règles du visible.

La rencontre entre Gianni Motti et les représentants d'extraterrestres est également éloquente. L'image du petit homme vert hystérique qui agite frénétiquement son pistolet laser et casse tout sur son passage est dépassée. Depuis plusieurs décennies déjà, l'extraterrestre ressemble à s'y méprendre à l'être humain. Soit l'homme a été cloné selon un modèle d'extraterrestre, soit l'extraterrestre a pris l'apparence de l'être humain. Cette dernière option est fascinante : elle éclaire tout un pan de l'art actuel. Seuls quelques minces indices trahissent l'extraterrestre (un auriculaire un peu raide par exemple, pour les besogneux de bas étage). Sitôt identifié, il recouvre son statut d'*alien*. Mais s'il disparaît de notre quotidien, a-t-il pour autant quitté notre réalité ? Peut-il vraiment s'éclipser *à l'extérieur* de la réalité ?

MULTIVERS, JEUX VIDÉO ET PHYSIQUE QUANTIQUE

Les extraterrestres ont une fonction bien précise : outre de nous divertir devant la télévision, ils nous aident à modeler une notion de réalité plus complexe que celle que le sens commun tente d'imposer. Si notre monde nous paraît plus réel qu'un autre, c'est qu'une telle impression découle non pas d'une expérience (car chaque monde apparaît à ses habitants comme l'unique réalité), mais d'une conception philosophique du monde qui historiquement s'est imposée au sens commun. [6]

Un autre acteur d'importance s'est immiscé dans la construction d'une notion plus expansive de la réalité : les jeux vidéos. Depuis l'avènement de ces derniers, tout joueur dispose désormais de plusieurs vies. De plus, il n'obtient pas une vie meilleure par une morale rigoureuse ou des rites respectés avec scrupule, mais par son agilité à se mouvoir dans l'univers qu'il se choisit.

Grâce à l'astronomie, la notion de réalité a évolué (ou plutôt s'est complexifiée) à pas de géants. La première exoplanète a été observée il y a moins d'une décennie et aujourd'hui on en découvre presque tous les jours. Un tel développement entraîne un retournement complet de la fameuse hypothèse d'une vie hors du système solaire. Etant donné le nombre d'exoplanètes actuellement observées, les scientifiques doivent admettre que, statistiquement, l'hypothèse d'une vie présente dans l'exosphère a plus de chances de l'emporter que l'hypothèse d'une vie uniquement terrestre.

Mais c'est peut-être la physique quantique qui ouvre les perspectives les plus nouvelles sur la notion de réalité. Le professeur de physique quantique David Deutsch a démontré dans ses recherches que s'il peut y avoir plusieurs univers, il n'y a qu'une seule réalité. Dans un texte reproduit dans le présent ouvrage, Deutsch explique que la réalité ne doit pas être jugée par rapport à un univers, mais bien plutôt à un "multivers" : "La réalité se comporte comme un *multivers*, une entité énorme qui, à grande échelle, possède une structure correspondant à plusieurs copies de l'univers tel qu'il est décrit par la physique classique, mais qui, à plus petite échelle, est un système unique et unifié."[7] Interviewé par un journaliste de *Philosophy Now*, David Deutsch explique de manière plus approfondie sa réflexion sur les univers parallèles. Nous livrons ci-dessous un extrait assez long, mais qui met en évidence l'importance sur ce que l'on ne voit pas ou ne perçoit pas dans les multiples sphères du réel :

"Commençons par le monde microscopique, parce que c'est seulement au niveau microscopique que nous avons des preuves directes d'univers parallèles. Comme première étape du raisonnement, il faut constater que le comportement des particules lors de l'expérience dite de la "diffraction par simple fente"[8] signale la présence de processus que nous ne voyons pas, mais que nous pouvons détecter grâce aux interférences qui se répercutent sur ce que nous voyons. La deuxième étape montre que la complexité de cette partie invisible de l'univers microscopique est bien plus vaste que celle que nous voyons. Le meilleur exemple pour illustrer cela, c'est le calcul quantique, qui nous permet de montrer qu'un ordinateur quantique de taille moyenne peut réaliser des calculs d'une complexité énorme, bien plus complexe que tout l'univers visible et tous ses atomes que l'on peut voir, Et tout cela se passe à l'intérieur d'un ordinateur quantique composé, lui, de quelques centaines d'atomes seulement. La réalité est donc faite de bien plus de choses que ce que nous pouvons percevoir. Ce que nous voyons n'est qu'une infime partie de la réalité et, la plupart du temps, le reste n'a aucune incidence sur nous. Mais lors de ces expériences assez particulières, certaines de ces parties ont bel et bien une incidence sur nous, et ces parties sont même plus complexes que tout ce que nous voyons.

L'étape suivante nous montre que la mécanique quantique, telle que nous la connaissons, permet de décrire ces autres parties de la réalité : les parties que nous ne voyons pas, tout comme celles que nous voyons. Elle permet même de décrire l'interaction entre les deux et lorsque nous analysons la structure de la partie invisible, nous pouvons constater – de manière assez précise – que celle-ci est composée de nombreuses copies de la partie visible. Ce n'est pas qu'il y aurait un "autre univers" monolithique, qui serait très complexe et suivrait d'autres règles. La partie invisible se comporte à peu près de la même manière que la partie visible, sauf qu'elle contient plusieurs copies.

"C'est comme la découverte d'autres planètes ou d'autres galaxies. Ne connaissant au départ que la Voie Lactée, nous n'avons pas seulement découvert un nombre incalculable d'étoiles se trouvant bien au-delà de la Voie Lactée : il y a plus de galaxies dans le ciel qu'il n'y a d'étoiles dans la Voie Lactée. Nous avons également découvert que la plupart des étoiles situées en dehors de la Voie Lactée se regroupent en d'autres petites Voies Lactées. Et c'est exactement ce qu'il se passe avec les univers parallèles. Ce n'est évidemment qu'une analogie, mais elle est intéressante. Comme les étoiles et les galaxies, les parties invisibles de la réalité forment des groupes qui ressemblent aux parties visibles. Dans chacun de ces groupes, que nous appelons "univers parallèle", toutes les particules peuvent interagir entre elles, même si elles n'interagissent que très rarement avec les particules d'autres univers. Et elles interagissent entre elles de la même manière que celles qui interagissent dans notre univers visible. C'est pourquoi nous les appelons "univers". La raison pour laquelle nous les appelons "parallèles" est que ces univers interagissent très peu entre eux, comme s'il s'agissait de lignes parallèles qui ne se croisent pas. (Il s'agit-là d'une approximation, car il y a des phénomènes d'interférence qui les poussent à interagir très légèrement.) Donc, voilà la suite d'arguments qui, du parallélisme (qui par ailleurs est beaucoup moins controversé au niveau microscopique

qu'au niveau macroscopique), nous mène aux univers parallèles. D'un point de vue philosophique, je voudrais ajouter qu'il est incohérent d'affirmer qu'"il y a des copies parallèles de toutes les particules qui participent aux interactions microscopiques, mais qu'il
n'y a pas de copies parallèles de celles participant aux interactions macroscopiques". Ce
serait comme si on affirmait que quelqu'un pouvait doubler le nombre de centimes sur un
compte bancaire sans pour autant doubler le nombre de francs."[9]

D'après Deutsch, ce que nous voyons ne représente donc qu'une infime partie de la réalité.
La réalité ne s'arrête pas à ce que nous voyons ou percevons et ce qui nous échappe, ce
"reste", cet "invisible" constitue un territoire indéfini dans lequel s'opère une infinité de
regroupements qui s'organisent – selon les expériences des physiciens quantiques – de
la même manière que le monde visible. Ce sont dans ce sens des *copies* du monde visible,
d'où cette affirmation qui peut sembler absurde selon laquelle il existe une copie de soi-
même dans chaque univers, mais que la totalité des copies ne constitue qu'une seule
réalité.

Il est intéressant d'observer la manière dont les notions de réalité et d'invisible ont pu
évoluer en art et à quel point elles se rapprochent aujourd'hui des récentes préoccupa-
tions des physiciens. "Voir l'invisible" – la revendication de bien des artistes de la première
moitié du vingtième siècle – visait l'exploration de territoires qui échappaient au monde
visible. Ces territoires étaient alors considérés comme "au-delà du réel", comme *terra
incognita* que les artistes allaient défricher tels des explorateurs de l'inconscient. En art
comme ailleurs, les héros partaient à la conquête de nouvelles contrées dont ils se devaient
de revenir en rédempteurs : grâce à eux, la réalité gagnait de nouveaux espaces, elle
pouvait s'étendre et survivre. L'extraterrestre disposait d'armes infaillibles pour conquérir
la planète Terre, Superman maîtrisait la gravité pour sauver la planète Terre et l'artiste
disposait d'inspirations transcendantales pour dévoiler les multiples faces cachées de la
planète Terre. Planant au dessus de la réalité, des lois, des contingences physiques et
psychiques, tous trois pouvaient assigner au "simple mortel" une place précise au sein de
la réalité. "Voir l'invisible", c'était (dans le meilleur des cas) dévoiler des territoires vierges,
des zones nouvelles, des plates-formes à occuper. Mais c'était surtout désigner un point
précis, défini par ce qui échappait à notre notion de réalité, par ce qui paraissait au-delà
de notre perception ordinaire.

LE RÉEL : COMBIEN DE COUCHES ?

Tout autre se révèle l'art d'aujourd'hui, qui sans surprise suit la même évolution que celle des héros, des extraterrestres et de la physique quantique. On se souvient de la fameuse question de Staline "Le Pape : combien de divisions ?" De la même manière, on pourrait aujourd'hui se demander : "Le réel : combien de couches ?" Une question qui en appelle d'autres : "Jusqu'à quel point peut-on étirer la réalité avant qu'elle ne se déchire ? Combien de couches supplémentaires peut-on greffer sur la réalité avant qu'elle ne s'effondre ?" Aujourd'hui, de telles questions apparaissent aussi absurdes que celle posée jadis par Staline. En effet, plus le XXème siècle avançait, plus le réel manifestait sa complexité. Et plus on multipliait les efforts pour l'analyser, plus ce dernier faisait montre d'une incroyable élasticité révélant un corps indéchirable, extensible et pliable à volonté. "Il n'y a pas de point fixe dans l'univers" affirmait déjà Einstein. Face à ce terrible constat, il a fallu s'organiser. Si la délicate mission de dessiner les frontières précises où l'homme pouvait trouver sa place incombait autrefois aux surhommes de tout poil, la situation a radicalement changé depuis quelques décennies. Les héros actuels s'enrhument, ont des pellicules, surveillent leur poids, souffrent de la prostate, vont en prison et/ou meurent d'un cancer. A peu près comme tout le monde. Il ne reste plus que quelques romantiques utopiques pour croire à cette *Mission Impossible*. D'ordinaire, ils se recrutent dans les milieux sportifs (pour courir le plus longtemps ou conduire le plus vite), para sportif (pour faire le tour du monde en ballon ou la traversée de l'Arctique) ou dans ceux du cinéma (pour incarner Jésus ou ses avatars, spécialistes de la rédemption en tous genres, tels Napoléon, Gandhi, Kennedy ou Jim Morrison). Mais ils ne font pas illusion longtemps. Surpris en train de sniffer de la coke, de contourner le fisc, de se gratter le bas ventre ou de lire un catalogue IKEA, ils sont tôt ou tard trahis par leur condition humaine.

Il faut s'y faire : il devient de plus en plus difficile de vivre par procuration. Les candidats à la déification ne manquent certes pas, mais aucun ne tient le coup plus d'une saison. Face à cette carence, les limites de la réalité s'effacent, aussi inexorablement que le désert avance. D'où la grande angoisse des philosophes d'aujourd'hui : le présent glisse à la surface du temps, rendant impossible l'appréhension d'un réel constitué de repères temporels clairement délimités. Immergés dans un temps mondial, nous assistons à une compression du passé, présent et futur et sommes embarqués dans l'immédiateté, l'instantanéité. Dominé par la notion de "temps réel", le présent ne peut que *passer* [10], dans un mouvement de transit continu, de glissement perpétuel. Certains philosophes tels que Virilio par exemple s'inquiètent d'une telle situation, marquée par l'éclatement des repères temporels traditionnels, où l'homme ne peut plus (et ne veut plus) freiner ce transfert permanent et perd tout espoir de retrouver des gestes susceptibles de fonder sa condition d'être-au-monde. Comment vivre dans un univers dépourvu de limites, alors que la recherche même de ces limites détermine un acte constitutif de notre équilibre ? Un tel paradoxe est au cœur des réflexions partagées par les humanistes de tout bord.

Généralement considérée comme un obstacle à surmonter, un mal à éradiquer, cette *mise en glisse* du monde constitue pour l'art un fantastique défi. Loin de s'en éloigner, l'art actuel s'y associe et adopte la même dynamique. Abandonnant au passé toute velléité de construire de nouvelles plateformes, ne croyant plus aux vertus des espaces "entre-deux" qui ont parsemé l'art des années 1990, les artistes d'aujourd'hui s'engagent dans une activité qui peut sembler laborieuse, voire dangereuse. "Un combat perdu d'avance" se lamenteront leurs parents, en secouant la tête. On rétorquera en citant la fameuse formule de Ben, "L'art est un sale boulot, mais il faut bien que quelqu'un le fasse". Les artistes poussent à l'extrême cette propension à se laisser aller, à ne plus résister à l'avancée du désert, à se laisser happer par cette vague déferlante qui brouille toute piste, toute limite. Non pas qu'ils aient décidé d'éteindre la télévision, d'arrêter de fumer et de se concentrer sur les *vraies* valeurs de notre société. Non, ils regardent le *Loft* en buvant des bières, font la grasse matinée et lisent les journaux de boulevards. Mais plutôt que de subir cet état de fait et de se révolter chaque premier de l'An en se disant "cette année je change", ils plongent au cœur de cette mise en glisse, tel des parasites adoptant le mode de fonctionnement de leurs hôtes. Le travail de Peter Fischli / David Weiss constitue à cet égard un modèle exemplaire.

Suite au prochain épisode

Épisode 16
EN ATTENDANT DIMANCHE

En 1978, Peter Fischli/David Weiss visitent un grand magasin d'ameublement dans la banlieue zurichoise. Ils flânent longuement avant de s'arrêter – ébahis – devant un pouf marocain. Une année plus tard, ils entament une collaboration artistique dont on mesure, vingt-cinq ans après, l'extraordinaire richesse et inventivité.

Analyser l'œuvre de Peter Fischli/David Weiss peut susciter un sentiment de vertige comparable aux enchaînements et aux mouvements dynamiques de leur célèbre film *Der Lauf der Dinge* (1987) : chaque chose est la cause de celle qui suit, tout objet est englobé dans une réaction en chaîne et cette succession effrénée semble ne connaître aucune fin, ne se fixer sur aucun concept précis, voire même identifiable.

Quel est le lien causal entre une tranche de mortadelle, une conduite d'égout, un bonhomme de neige, un chou-fleur, un paysage en béton, un cornichon en équilibre sur une carotte, un pain, une locomotive, le tarmac d'un aéroport, des fleurs multicolores, un seau en polyuréthane, les pyramides égyptiennes ?

En 1984 [11], Peter Fischli/David Weiss établissent un inventaire des questions à résoudre en priorité : "*Est-ce que tout n'est qu'une question de temps ? Dois-je changer les draps du lit ? Y a-t-il une vie dans l'espace ? Est-ce que l'on m'aime ? Jusqu'où peut-on aller ? Peut-on faire tout faux ? Encore un petit verre ?*"

Où sont les réponses ? Peter Fischli sourit et parle d'une "schizophrénie des sentiments". On pourrait ajouter : une mise en glisse des sensations. Car qui regarde vraiment leurs images, par exemple ces photographies volontairement banales intitulées *Bilder, Ansichten* (1991)? Elles montrent ce que tout le monde connaît, ce qui est inscrit de manière collective dans la mémoire visuelle. Voir, et montrer, ce que le sens commun attend d'une illustration rassurante, d'une belle image, quelque chose que l'on déchiffre immédiatement et dont les clefs de lecture sont unanimement partagées.[12] Des images archétypiques. Les pyramides, les aéroports, les couchers de soleil sur une plage, la Tour Eiffel, un chaton à peine né, des pommes rouges gorgées de soleil, le Cervin, le Grand Canyon. Des images que l'on a vues mille fois sur toutes les cartes postales du monde et dont même John Waters, le prince du mauvais goût, s'est demandé "qui a été le premier à dire du bien d'*Airports*"[13], avant de confesser qu'il voyait dans ces clichés un nouveau type de beauté, un nouveau type d'œuvre d'art dont il n'y a strictement rien à dire. Voir une fois encore le Cervin ou un coucher de soleil n'est pas désagréable. Et de toute façon on ne regarde plus vraiment ces images que l'on a depuis toujours sous les yeux. On *glisse* dessus pour penser à autre chose. Aux vacances de l'année passée, dans ce merveilleux chalet. A cette série télévisée que l'on regardait en famille.

MEUBLER LE TEMPS. ÉLOGE DE LA LENTEUR ET ESTHÉTIQUE DU GLISSEMENT

Ces photographies ne sont pas *ready made*. Peter Fischli / David Weiss ne se sont pas contentés de puiser dans une vaste banque de données les images qui semblaient à leurs yeux les plus significatives. Le voyage, la flânerie, l'attente du moment le plus opportun, le désir de réussir des clichés n'ayant rien à envier aux plus belles cartes postales constituent des éléments bien plus importants. Cette volonté d'éprouver la puissance et l'aura acquises par le ready made se retrouve dans des travaux d'une nature complètement différente, comme par exemple *Der Tisch* (1992). Sur un immense plateau en bois se retrouvent pêle-mêle les objets les plus hétéroclites, du produit de nettoyage à la pâtée pour chien, en passant par des pots de peinture, des briques, du chocolat, des tabourets, des pinceaux, des bidons, un téléphone, une canette de Coca, etc. Il pourrait s'agir d'un ensemble d'objets se trouvant dans l'atelier des artistes, à cette différence près que les éléments exposés sur la table ont tous été méticuleusement fabriqués en polyuréthane, un matériau que les artistes ont utilisé dès leur début. D'autres travaux ont été effectués en gomme noire, comme ce pouf marocain réalisé en 1987. Un *ready made* ne se fabrique pas, il apparaît subitement, transfiguré d'un état à un autre. Comme l'a relevé Boris Groys[14] dans un essai passionnant, l'œuvre d'art a atteint au cours du siècle dernier la vitesse de la lumière, puisque sa production est aussi rapide que la pensée et ne dépend que d'une prise de décision. Peter Fischli / David Weiss proposent quant à eux une vaste entreprise de décélération. Les travaux qu'ils élaborent ne se distinguent en rien de nos objets quotidiens. On s'attend à trouver des éléments manufacturés, indices de notre époque machiniste. On découvre des objets "faits main", exécutés avec la lenteur propre au travail artisanal. Il ne s'agit pas pour Peter Fischli / David Weiss d'exalter les vertus de l'artisan. La lenteur est reliée au temps et pour eux "le travail assidu est du temps gaspillé utilement". La lenteur peut aussi être celle de la flânerie, de la promenade. Elle est alors liée à cette question existentielle : comment meubler le temps efficacement ? Que faire un dimanche après-midi ? Que voit-on lorsque l'on flâne ? En général rien de particulier. On se promène dans un décor qui nourrit notre rêve éveillé.

C'est dans ce "rien de particulier" que sont intervenus Peter Fischli / David Weiss avec une œuvre présentant sur douze moniteurs plus de 80 heures de vidéo (XLVI Biennale de Venise, 1995). Les artistes ont filmé le trajet entre leur domicile et l'atelier, une excursion dans les Alpes, une course de motocross en salle, la fabrication du fromage. A Zurich, ils continuent de flâner et regardent les gens laver leur voitures, acheter une saucisse à un stand. Aucun commentaire n'est donné. Aucune volonté de se démarquer d'une esthétique télévisuelle neutre. L'ensemble rappelle bien les séquences "No Comment" d'Euronews. Mais rien ne se passe. Personne ne tire dans la foule. Les artistes filment tout simplement ce qui les intéresse sur le moment. Lorsque l'on meuble le temps, on est à l'affût du moindre événement. On établit une hiérarchie des choses intéressantes. On choisit de suivre une scène, même la plus anodine, au détriment d'une autre. On attend que "quelque chose se passe" et dans la vie comme dans les vidéos de Peter Fischli / David Weiss, il se passe rarement quelque chose. Alors on attend. Et cette attente de l'essentiel constitue souvent l'essentiel à attendre. On attend dimanche avec impatience. Le dimanche – c'est bien connu – on s'ennuie, et c'est finalement cette attente qui se révèle le moment le plus passionnant.

Peter Fischli / David Weiss ont goût à la flânerie. Ils ont photographié pendant une année des fleurs, des champignons et des jardins potagers en recourant à une technique de débutant : la double exposition. Le résultat est confondant. "Que c'est beau !" s'exclame-t-on spontanément, alors que dans le même temps se manifeste l'esprit critique, soucieux de ne pas se laisser impressionner. Cette double exposition des beautés naturelles engendre des sentiments ambigus et rappelle "l'esthétique de la schizophrénie" évoquée plus haut. Dans une installation présentée pour la première fois en 1999[15],

Peter Fischli / David Weiss projettent ces images contre les cimaises. Grâce à une technique de fondu-enchaîné, chaque diapositive – résultat d'une double exposition – chevauche la suivante, alimenté par un carrousel au flux ininterrompu. Cette quadruple exposition est vertigineuse. Face à l'absence totale de points fixes, l'œil ne peut que glisser sur les images. La vue chancelle, grisée par cette illusion du mouvement continu auquel le cinéma nous a habitué. Elle n'expérimente plus la notion d'observation, mais celle de *trajet*. Or, contrairement au cinéma, nous assistons à un trajet sans but, sans début ni fin, un trajet qui n'est que passage. Et comme leurs images qui défilent en se super-posant, les artistes ne font que passer.

Contrairement aux protagonistes du Land Art quittant leur atelier pour arpenter *on the road* les gigantesques étendues américaines à la recherche d'un site à investir, les artistes d'aujourd'hui n'investissent plus rien du tout. Ils ne partent pas en expédition, ils se promènent. Ils ne se positionnent plus face au paysage, ils se glissent à l'intérieur de celui-ci. La promenade recèle une vertu efficace et salvatrice : elle meuble le temps. Et plutôt que de subir le mouvement de transit continu qui constitue notre "temps réel", elle permet aux artistes de s'adapter à la vitesse imposée par l'instantanéité de notre présent et d'élaborer une véritable *esthétique du glissement*.

PAR ORDRE D'APPARITION

CAPTAIN WILLARD – MIKE TYSON – L'ADVERSAIRE – LES SPECTATEURS – LES ARTISTES – L'AUTOMOBILISTE
MISS BLACK AMERICA – L'ARBITRE – LE GARDE DU CORPS – LE SPORTIF – SARAH TYSON – COLIN POWELL
BEN LADEN – L'EXTRATERRESTRE – JOHN WAYNE – LE VOISIN DE PALIER – GIANNI MOTTI
ROSEMARIE TROCKEL – LES JAPONAIS ET LEUR GUIDE – LES RAËLIENS – FITZCARRALDO – UMBERTO ECO
COLUMBO – DERRICK – SUPERMAN – DAVID DEUTSCH – STALINE – LE PAPE – EINSTEIN – JÉSUS
NAPOLÉON – GANDHI – KENNEDY – JIM MORRISON – VIRILIO – BEN – PETER FISCHLI / DAVID WEISS
JOHN WATERS – BORIS GROYS

[1] Marc-Olivier Wahler, *Transfert. Art dans l'espace urbain*, Transfert, Bienne, 2000, p. 29. Le concept de furtivité a été développé par Alexandre Szames dans un article intitulé "Esthétique de la furtivité" in *5, 6, 7, 8, 9 CAN*, CAN, Neuchâtel, 2000, p. 42. (Ce texte, écrit en 1998-1999, reprend certaines thèses développées par l'auteur dans "Esthétique de la furtivité", in *Crash*, n°2, mars-avril 1998.)

[2] Wallace Matthews, journaliste au *New York Post*. Cité par Fred Hirzel dans un article (*Le Temps*, Rubrique Sports, jeudi 14 mars 2002) commentant le feu vert obtenu par Mike Tyson le 13 mars 2002 pour remonter sur le ring. Le terme "bête de l'Apocalypse" lui est emprunté.

[3] "She is an avid golfer, helps steer FOCA and creates gourmet meals. She is married to Mike Tyson and has both ears. Sarah has been a docent at SITE Santa Fe for five years." http://www.sitesantafe.org/general/contacts.html

[4] Gilles Lipovetsky, *L'ère du vide*, Gallimard, Paris, 1983, p. 107.

[5] Umberto Eco, "Conclusion 1993", in *De Superman au surhomme*, Grasset, Paris, 1993, p. 210. Cité par Marc-Olivier Wahler dans *Transfert. Art dans l'espace urbain*, p. 29, Transfert, Bienne, 2000.

[6] Lire la correspondance entre David Deutsch et Seth Loyd, "Are parallel universes equally real? Brain tennis: David Deutsch vs Seth Loyd", Originally published 9 July 1997 on http://hotwired.lycos.com/synapse. Cette correspondance est reproduite dans le présent ouvrage, pp. 50-58.

[7] Idem, page 50-58.

[8] Ndt: la diffraction est un phénomène qui montre le lien entre deux ondes rencontrant un obstacle. Ce phénomène est guidé par le Principe d'Huygens: tous les points d'un front d'onde agissent comme une source de plus petite longueur d'onde et se propagent à la même vitesse que l'onde dont ils sont issus.

[9] Filiz Peach, entretien avec David Deutsch, in *Philosophy Now*, Nr. 30, décembre 2000.

[10] "Ce monde tel que nous le voyons est en train de passer", Paul de Tarse, cité par Paul Virilio, *Esthétique de la disparition*, Galilée, Paris 1989, page 9.

[11] *Fragentopf*. Les questions sont inscrites au fond d'un vase en polyuréthane.

[12] "Impossible de savoir s'ils font des photos pour se souvenir du voyage ou s'ils font le voyage pour prendre des photos" (Christophe Domino, "Petite encyclopédie portative", in *Peter Fischli / David Weiss*, Musée national d'art moderne, Centre Georges Pompidou, Paris, 1992.

[13] John Waters, "Airports", in *Vogue*, New York, 1990.

[14] Boris Groys, "The Speed of Art", in *Peter Fischli / David Weiss*. *XLVI Biennale di Venezia*, OFC, Berne, 1995.

[15] Musée d'art moderne de la Ville de Paris.

S I

SWISS INSTITUTE NEW YORK
JANUARY 2001 – DECEMBER 2003

MAIN EXHIBITIONS

UNDER PRESSURE WITH CERCLE RAMO NASH, MARTIN CREED, SIMONE DECKER, GRAHAM DURWARD, FABRICE GYGI, ERIC HATTAN, @HOME, PIERRE JOSEPH, LANG/BAUMANN, STÉPHANE MAGNIN, THOM MERRICK, TAKASHI MURAKAMI, PHILIPPE PARRENO, STEFAN PENTE, HENRIK PLENGE JAKOBSEN, PIERRE REIMER, ROMAN SIGNER / **GIANNI MOTTI** WITH THE VATICAN SWISS GUARDS AND AS AN ASSISTANT OF ROBERT BARRY, MAURIZIO CATTELAN, JESSICA DIAMOND, SYLVIE FLEURY, THOMAS HIRSCHHORN, PIERRE HUYGHE, KAREN KILIMNIK, SOL LEWITT, JULIAN OPIE, KRISTIN OPPENHEIM, PHILIPPE PARRENO, UGO RONDINONE, NANCY RUBIN, LILY VAN DER STOKKER, RIRKRIT TIRAVANIJA, ROSEMARIE TROCKEL, HEIMO ZOBERNIG / **SISLEJ XHAFA** WITH SLOT MACHINES / **FABRICE GYGI** WITH A POLLING STATION / **MAYDAY MAYDAY** WITH RENÉ BAUERMEISTER, PETER GARFIELD, TIM & FRANTISKA GILMAN, BOB GRAMSMA, NAOYA HATAKEYAMA, ON KAWARA, PETER LAND, ABIGAIL LANE, EUAN MACDONALD, THOM MERRICK, JAN VAN OOST, SOPHY RICKETT, JEAN-CLAUDE RUGGIRELLO, SONTEXT, JORDAN TINKER / **CHRISTIAN JANKOWSKI** WITH A MAGICIAN, CHILDREN, AND CUSTOMS OFFICERS

OTHER EXHIBITIONS

OLAF BREUNING / TONY MATELLI / ALBERTO GIACOMETTI / LANG/BAUMANN / LORI HERSBERGER / JONATHAN MONK / JANINE GORDON, LUDOVIC JECKER / SPIROS MARGARIS / GELATIN / OLAV WESTPHALEN / DANIEL PFLUMM / RODERICK BUCHANAN / URI TZAIG / ERIC HATTAN

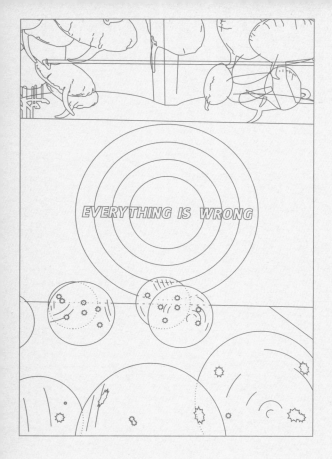

UNDER PRESSURE

CERCLE RAMO NASH, MARTIN CREED, SIMONE DECKER, GRAHAM DURWARD,
FABRICE GYGI, ERIC HATTAN, PIERRE JOSEPH, LANG/BAUMANN, STÉPHANE MAGNIN,
THOM MERRICK, TAKASHI MURAKAMI, PHILIPPE PARRENO, STEFAN PENTE,
HENRIK PLENGE JAKOBSEN, PIERRE REIMER, ROMAN SIGNER, @HOME

JANUARY 25 - MARCH 3, 2001

TALK IS CHEAP
GIANNI MOTTI AND SISLEJ XHAFA
APRIL 5 – MAY 19, 2001

UNTITLED (PREVIOUSLY CALLED MAYDAY MAYDAY)

RENÉ BAUERMEISTER, PETER GARFIELD, BOB GRAMSMA, NAOYA HATAKEYAMA,
ON KAWARA, PETER LAND, ABIGAIL LANE, EUAN MACDONALD, THOM MERRICK,
JAN VAN OOST, SOPHY RICKETT, JEAN-CLAUDE RUGGIRELLO, SONTEXT,
JORDAN TINKER

SEPTEMBER 13 – OCTOBER 20, 2001

CHRISTIAN JANKOWSKI
NOVEMBER 15, 2001 - JANUARY 12, 2002

MAIN EXHIBITIONS

LORI HERSBERGER WITH MOVIES SUCH AS *DJANGO, DIE HARD, EXCALIBUR, RONIN, EL TOPO, THE SEARCHERS* / **UGO RONDINONE** WITH **JOHN GIORNO** AND **URS FISCHER** / OLAF BREUNING WITH REAL DOLL/ JIM SHAW WITH A NEW RELIGION/ **STEVEN PARRINO** AND **JUTTA KOETHER** WITH BLACK DICE, FOOT, CHRISTIAN MARCLAY, MERZBOW

OTHER EXHIBITIONS

MICHAEL ROSS / MARIA MARSHALL / ANNEMARIE SCHWARZENBACH / YVES NETZHAMMER / ERIK PARKER / FIA BACKSTRÖM / BLAIR THURMAN / SOPHIE BERNARD / MAI-THU PERRET / KIM GORDON / VALENTIN CARRON / **ONE DAY** WITH REBECCA BIRD, BECKET BOWES, EHDEE CHU, TIM & FRANTISKA GILMAN, BETH HOWE, PAUL JACOBSEN, CRIS MOSS, FRANK OLIVE, BRETT CODY ROGERS, JESS SEGALL AND TONI SERRATELLI

LECTURES

CHRISTIAN JANKOWSKI / OLAV WESTPHALEN / BICE CURIGER / JIM SHAW

HOW CAN YOU KILL ME? (I'M ALREADY DEAD)
LORI HERSBERGER

JANUARY 24 – MARCH 9, 2002

LOWLAND LULLABY
UGO RONDINONE WITH JOHN GIORNO AND URS FISCHER
MARCH 26 – MAY 11, 2002

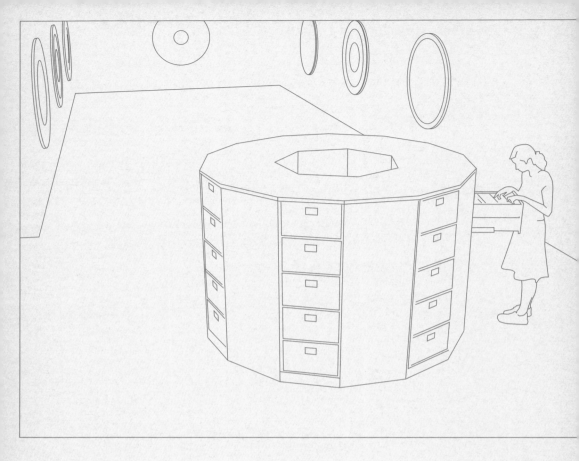

THE GOODMAN IMAGE FILE AND STUDY
JIM SHAW
SEPTEMBER 14 – OCTOBER 26, 2002

BLACK BONDS
JUTTA KOETHER AND STEVEN PARRINO
NOVEMBER 12 2002 - JANUARY 4, 2003

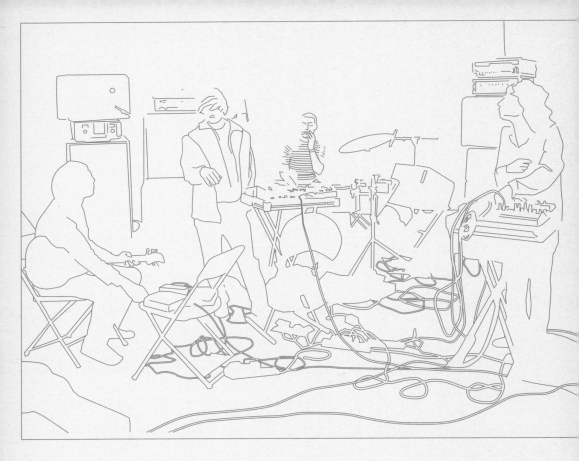

BLACK BONDS
PERFORMANCE BY BLACK DICE
DECEMBER 17, 2002

2003 ←

MAIN EXHIBITIONS

ERIC HATTAN / **EXTRA** WITH VIRGINIE BARRÉ, OLIVIER
BLANCKART, STÉPHANE DAFFLON, WIM DELVOYE,
PETER FISCHLI/DAVID WEISS, SYLVIE FLEURY, DANIEL
FIRMAN, GIANNI MOTTI, BRUNO PEINADO, ROMAN
SIGNER / **DUST MEMORIES** WITH MEL BOCHNER,
JORDI COLOMER, JEAN DUPUY, TOM FRIEDMAN,
JONATHAN HOROWITZ, JONATHAN MONK, BOB MORRIS,
PIET MONDRIAN, CORNELIA PARKER, CLAUDIO
PARMIGGIANI, DAVID POISSENOT, DARIO ROBLETO,
MICHAEL ROSS, LAWRENCE WIENER, ERWIN WURM,
CURATED BY EMMANUEL LATREILLE / **NIC HESS** /
ERWIN WURM / **THE LAST PAINTING SHOW**,
CURATED BY OLIVIER MOSSET

OTHER EXHIBITIONS

LIQUID SKY WITH CHRISTOPH BÜCHEL-BOB GRAMSMA,
DEBORA WARNER, TONY MATELLI (AT FRAC
BOURGOGNE, FRANCE) / ZOE LEONARD / MICHEL
FRANÇOIS / EHDEE CHU, AND MUCH MORE!

UNDER PRESSURE

"A group exhibition [that] may simply raise your spirits."
→ Kim Levin, *The Village Voice*, February 20, 2001

"This season's most obsessively focused group show."
→ Robert Mahoney, *Time Out New York*, March 1, 2001

TALK IS CHEAP. GIANNI MOTTI AND SISLEJ XHAFA

"Two maverick artists, whose M.O.'s cross the line where life and art meet luck and magic."
→ Kim Levin, *The Village Voice*, April 24, 2001

"Until recently Xhafa's work has been seen only in European venues, but a current show at Swiss Institute in New York has provided the artist with his first significant exposure in the United States."
→ Giorgio Verzotti, *Artforum*, May 2001

FABRICE GYGI

"Over all, the spare installation seems like some collaboration between Franz Kafka and Donald Judd."
→ *The New Yorker*, August 20, 2001

"Fabrice Gygi's new installation should tweak a few raw nerves."
→ Michael Wilson, *Artforum.com*, July 2001

UNTITLED (previously called MAYDAY MAYDAY)

"This 14-artist exhibition about fateful moments and pure panic (...) raises questions of relevance, irrelevance, coincidence, and the sometimes uncanny prescience of art."
→ Kim Levin, *The Village Voice*, October 3, 2001

"A surprising group show curated by Marc-Olivier Wahler. Somehow influenced by David Lynch (...), the strength of Untitled relies on the visionary qualities of the works and lets the viewers come up with their favorite drama."
→ Massimiliano Gioni, *Flash Art*, November/December, 2001

CHRISTIAN JANKOWSKI

"Christian Jankowski (...) is a sweetheart. Like Rirkrit Tiravanija and Gillian Wearing, he takes the relatively cold matter of Conceptual Art and melds it into something warm but not gooey funny but not satirical. He doesn't so much critique society as mingle with it and occasionally tactfully collaborate with it. (...) Its three video works include one of the season's hits."
→ Roberta Smith, *The New York Times*, January 4, 2002

HOW CAN YOU KILL ME? (I'M ALREADY DEAD)
LORI HERSBERGER

"On three big screens, this Swiss artist projects montages of Hollywood movie clips, mostly moments of suspense or climatic violence from disaster films, Westerns, police thrillers and war movies. Through abrupt cutting and repetition of loud soundtracks as well as imagery, Mr. Hersberger creates an unnerving delirium while raising questions about our appetite for stories of death and apocalyptic destruction."
→ Ken Johnson, *The New York Times*, February 15, 2002

"(...) The gallery, dimmed to accommodate three floor-to-ceiling film projections, is a whirling centrifuge of brutal sadistic and ruefully cliché clips: Hersberger has harvested grand denouements from sources as disparate as spaghetti Westerns, Bruce Willis action flicks, and end-of-the-world epics. These images are linked only by their moments of utter calamity, and by the artist's short-shrift cuts to scenes that audiences usually wait through an entire movie to see (...). Hersberger's editing technique highlights the visual and acoustic opulence of these sequences, which in turn emphasizes the materiality of film- and nearly renders the medium sculptural (...). There is certainly no illusion of a "safe haven" here among the wreckage, but (and perhaps this is Hersberger's point) we're still happy to hang out and watch."
→ Johanna Burton, *Time Out New York*, February 28, 2002

LOWLAND LULLABY
UGO RONDINONE WITH JOHN GIORNO AND URS FISCHER

"Dreamed up by Swiss mavericks Ugo Rondinone and Urs Fischer and the seminal New York spoken-word poet John Giorno, "Lowland Lullaby" won my award for surreal collaboration of the year. From beneath Rondinone's Op art-decorated, stagelike platform floor emanated a recording of Giorno reading his epic poem "There Was a Bad Tree," which provided accompaniment for Fischer's loopy drawings and sculptures. Like the Swiss Institute's inspiringly strange programming, "Lowland Lullaby" made absolute sense and no sense at all."
→ Matthew Higgs, *Artforum*, Best of 2002, 2002

HELLO DARKNESS
OLAF BREUNING

"(...) You step through the hole into a vast dark space ani-
mated by ominous music and a slowly spinning wheel of
blue light (...). A dialogue between death and the maiden
sounds like a loopy conversation between Darth Vader
and Linda Blair in "The Exorcist" (...). This all makes for
amusingly over-the-top and, for a moment at least, grip-
ping theater."
→ Ken Johnson, *The New York Times*, June 21, 2002
(New York Times star for "highly recommended show")

"(...) What Breuning excels at is glam-trash cliché, willful
crudity, pretensions of profundity, and special effects."
→ Kim Levin, *The Village Voice*, Voice Choice Shortlist,
July 2, 2002

THE GOODMAN IMAGE FILE AND STUDY
JIM SHAW

"Jim Shaw, the California conceptualist, who in his art
often pretends to be someone else, usually a bad painter,
now gives us an artist named Adam O. Goodman, a be-
liever in a made-up religion, O-ism (...). At the Swiss Institute, then, we find his (that is, Goodman's) circular
paintings and also file cabinets (arranged in a circle or O)
containing tacky yellowing magazine and newspaper clip-
pings that he (that is, Gunn, who is really Goodman, who
is, of course, Mr. Shaw) uses for his illustrations. All very
funny. (...) The whole project is, as usual with Mr. Shaw,
a sly, sardonic take on the mythologies of American art
and high-low taste, raised to a clever pitch by his obses-
sive, black-humored, distinctly absurd sensibility."
→ Michael Kimmelman, *The New York Times*,
October 4, 2002

BLACK BONDS. MERZBOW

"(...) Japan's Masami Akita, a.k.a. Merzbow, has managed
to turn antiart premise of creating sound with broken
equipment into a platform for more than 20 years of rigorous production (...). Counting at least 150 records in
his discography, topped off by 2001's 50-CD Merzbox,
Akita has gained near ubiquity among record collectors
and chronicles of underground culture (...). While not
known for any particular live theatrics, the sheer intensity of Merzbow's music should make for a compelling
performance. The Swiss Institute show, in particular,
will take place amid a display of "failed" paintings by Jutta
Koether and Steven Parrino. Koether's works look like
an explosion in a black-paint factory, but they also repay
closer looking, as neatly scripted apothegms are written
onto the canvas. Similarly, Merzbow's music springs from
failure or unintended results of the artistic process, but
also rewards attention. Despite its forbidding surface, it
offers a lot of finer detail, and the appreciation of small
differences and gradual changes becomes the basis for
the listening experience."
→ Bob Bannister, *Time Out New York*,
December 5-12, 2002

LIQUID CONCRETE. ERIC HATTAN

"Eric Hattan's New York debut escapes with its life,
squeaking past the threat of an increasingly generic
format: a tangle of video monitors flickering with brief
scenes of everyday life. But Mr. Hattan, who is Swiss,
seems to specialize in such scrapes (...). His brief loops,
one to a monitor, capture the daily choreography of
people and things (mostly things), played out in fleeting
instances of random beauty, odd coincidence and benign
violence that occur at the periphery of vision or consciousness (...). Casual yet oddly concentrated, Mr.
Hattan's little vignettes evoke the tradition of street pho-
tography and amateur snapshots, as well as Situationist
Art's fabled "drift" through the urban environment."
→ Roberta Smith, *The New York Times*,
January 24, 2003

The Swiss Institute – Contemporary Art is grateful
to all of the institutions, corporations, and individuals
mentioned below who support its efforts.

SI CORPORATE SUPPORTERS 2002 / 2003

Bank Julius Baer & Co. Ltd.
Bobst Group Inc.
Breitling USA, Inc.
Credit Suisse First Boston
Davidoff of Geneva (CT) Inc.
The Edelman Companies
Gibney, Anthony & Flaherty, LLP
Nestlé USA, Inc.
Novartis Corporation
O'Connor Davies Munns Dobbins, LLP
Panalpina
Partners Group (USA) Inc.
Ringier AG
Rolex Watch U.S.A., Inc.
Sika Corporation
Swiss International Air Lines SA
Swiss Reinsurance America Corp.
UBS Warburg
USM Modular Furniture
Wuersch & Gering LLP
Zenith Watches USA

SI PUBLIC CONTRIBUTORS
INCLUDING FOUNDATIONS 2001– 2003

Bundesamt für Kultur / BAK
(Swiss Federal Office of Culture)
Pro Helvetia (Arts Council of Switzerland)
PRS Presence Switzerland

Stanley Thomas Johnson Foundation
AFAA
Étant Donnés
Kanton Basel-Stadt, Kulturabteilung
Eidgenössisches Departement für
Auswärtige Angelegenheiten (EDA) / Kulturfonds
Consulate General of Switzerland, New York
Cultural Services of the French Embassy, New York
Flemish Community of Belgium
Fondation Nestlé pour l'Art
Fonds cantonal de décoration et d'art visuel, Geneva
Fondation Suisa
SwissPeaks Festival

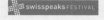

→ S I MEMBERSHIP

To foster the cultural dialogue between the Swiss and
the many other communities and nationalities found in
New York City, the SI depends on the
support of our Members as well as on public and corporate funding.

In becoming a Member, you will join a community that
revolves around our schedule of exciting events.
Membership categories are divided into a series of levels,
allowing everyone the opportunity to contribute to the SI
in the manner they desire. For further membership information please visit www.swissinstitute.net. To join the SI
please e-mail us at info@swissinstitute.net.

→ S I MEMBERS 2002/2003

A4 Studio, Uschi Weissmueller
Fabienne P. Abrecht and Charles Abrecht
Kurt E. Ackermann
Nathalie Angles
Regula Aregger and Ted Hepp
Ambassador Roger Bär
Roger L. Bahnik
Jean M. H. Bauer
Susanna E. Bedell
Marcel Biedermann
Emil Biemann
Anita and Hans Binkert
Ariane M. Braillard
Maya S. Brassel
Thomas Andreas Bühler and Rosemarie Schiller-Bühler
Gertrude Chandler
Clock Wise Productions, Inc., Nina Froriep
Hildy Crosser
Arianne Kaitrene Culley
Ambassador Alfred Defago
Asher B. Edelman
Malcolm Edgar
Hans C. Egloff
Michael Fankhauser and Andrea Fankhauser
Astrid Fitzgerald
Jeffrey E. Freedman
Hans and Barbara Frei
Lea Freid/Lombard-Freid Fine Arts
Ben Frija
J. Ormond Frost and Rita Robert Frost
Globe Language Services, Steven Berkowitz and
George R. Fletcher, Ed.D.
Edward M. Gomez
Evi Gorsch
Dieter von Graffenried and Carolina Nitsch
Paolo Grassi
George Gyssler
Heidi Haas
Dieter Hall
Richard Hahnloser
Catherine Hauck
Jacqueline Heer
Frank W. Hoch and. Lisina M. Hoch
Ursula Hodel
Theodore U. Horger
Jean-Marc Houmard
Max Imgrüth
Hans Kaeser
Margrit Kaeser and Hansrudolf Kaeser
Andromahi Kefalos
Ruth Kimche
George Klein
Eduard K. Kleiner and Rayanne Kleiner
Rona Richter-Krauthammer and Michael Krauthammer
Thomas and Ute Krayenbuehl
Hans-Rudolf Küchler
Cornelia Kueng and Hans Kueng
Heinz W. Kunz
Annette Kym and Klaus Drexl

Ueli Laupper
Frederic Levrat
Eric Lomas
Ambassador Raymond Loretan and
Mrs. Carol de Quay Loretan
Oliver Lutz
Lucille Maffia
Alice E. Maloof
Audrey Manley
Edward P. and Maya Manley
Christian Marclay
Trudi Mathys
Marie Louise McHugh
Mission of Switzerland to the United Nations
Claire Montgomery & James MacGregor
Hans R. Mosimann and Marcia J. Mosimann
Olivier C. Mosset
Bob Nickas
George E. Paltzer
Jeffrey Peek
Robert Perret, Jr.
Process Tech. Corp., Robert L. Rorschach
Prounmedia, LLC, and Matthew Becker
B. de Quervain
Jennifer Re and Thomas C. Re.
Beat F.K. Reinhart
Marion Meyer-Robboy
Gilbert M. Rolle
Nicolas Rossier
Edward Rudlinger
Eva Schicker
Elisabeth M. Schneier
Patricia Schramm and Frank Schramm
Guido Schuler and Elisabeth Schuler
Paolo Seiferle
Gregory Sholette
Daniel H. Sigg
Anne Katrin Spiess
Ambassador Jeno C.A. Staehelin
John Steigerwald
Hendel Teicher and Terry Winters
Louise Planck Terry
Dr. Christian Tschudi and Elisabetta Ullu
Rudolf Wassmer and Janine Wassmer
Simon Watson
Fiorimonde V. Wedekind
John W. Weeden
Richard Weiss
Erich Winkler and Nancy Allerston
Egon P.S. Zehnder
Peter Zehnder
Charles E. Ziegler

EXTRA THANKS →

THE ARTISTS AND CONTRIBUTORS

Fia Backström, Virginie Barré, Sophie Bernard, Rebecca
Bird, Black Dice, Olivier Blanckart, Mel Bochner, Becket
Bowes, Olaf Breuning, Roderick Buchanan, Christoph
Büchel, Valentin Carron, Cercle Ramo Nash, Ehdee Chu,
Jordi Colomer, Martin Creed, Bice Curiger, Stéphane
Dafflon, Simone Decker, Wim Delvoye, David Deutsch,
Jean Dupuy, Graham Durward, Daniel Firman, Urs
Fischer, Peter Fischli / David Weiss, Sylvie Fleury, Foot,
Michel François, Tom Friedman, Peter Garfield, Gelatin,
Alberto Giacometti, Tim & Frantiska Gilman, John Giorno,
Janine Gordon, Kim Gordon, Bob Gramsma, Fabrice Gygi,
Naoya Hatakeyama, Eric Hattan, Lori Hersberger, Nic
Hess, @Home, Jonathan Horowitz, Beth Howe, Paul
Jacobsen, Christian Jankowski, Ludovic Jecker, Pierre
Joseph, Rolf Julius, On Kawara, Jutta Koether, Peter
Land, Abigail Lane, Lang/Baumann, Sloan Leblanc, Zoe
Leonard, Seth Lloyd, Euan Macdonald, Stéphane Magnin,
Christian Marclay, Spiros Margaris, Maria Marshall, Tony
Matelli, Thom Merrick, Merzbow, Jonathan Monk, Bob
Morris, Cris Moss, Olivier Mosset, Gianni Motti, Takashi
Murakami, Yves Netzhammer, Bob Nickas, Frank Olive,
Cornelia Parker, Erik Parker, Philippe Parreno, Steven
Parrino, Bruno Peinado, Stefan Pente, Mai-Thu Perret,
Henrik Plenge Jakobsen, Daniel Pflumm, David Poissenot,
Pierre Reimer, Sophy Rickett, Dario Robleto, Brett Cody
Rogers, Ugo Rondinone, Michael Ross, Jean-Claude
Ruggirello, Annemarie Schwarzenbach, Jess Segall,
Toni Serratelli, Jim Shaw, Roman Signer, Sontext, Blair
Thurman, Jordan Tinker, Uri Tzaig, Jan Van Oost, Debora
Warner, Lawrence Weiner, Olav Westphalen, Erwin
Wurm, Sislej Xhafa.

GALLERIES AND INSTITUTIONS

Galleries Spencer Brownstone, Paula Cooper, Gasser &
Grunert, Barbara Gladstone, I-20, Leo Koenig,
Maccarone, Matthew Marks, Metro Pictures, The New
York Kunsthalle, Sonnabend, Sperone Westwater, Team
Gallery, New York. The Fabric Workshop, Philadelphia.
Victoria Miro Gallery, London. Gallery Art & Public,
Mamco, Geneva. Galleries Hauser & Wirth & Presenhuber,
Bob van Orsouw, Zurich. Galleries Chantal Crousel,
Loevenbruck, Emmanuel Perrotin, Thaddaeus Ropac,
Paris. FRAC Bourgogne, Dijon. Art Basel, Basel / Miami.

INDIVIDUALS

Doina Adam, George Adam, Olivier Antoine, Jeremy
Benjamin, Monika Bergin, Christian Bernard, Caroline
Blaser, Jean-Christophe Blaser, Becket Bowes, Claudia
Carby, Paul Devautour, Manuella Denogent, Ainsley
Donald, Sonia Essebag, Aline Favre, Lukas Fitze, Karin
Frank, Chris Frey, Cordula Furrer, Bruno Gerber, John
Gernand, Bernard Gingras, Daniel Girod, Joe Grant,
André Güdel, MK Guth, Pierre Huber, Claude Joray, Peter
Jordi, Sam Keller, Pius Knüsel, Martin Kunz, Thomas
Laely, Uli Lang, Emmanuel Latreille, Hervé Loevenbruck,
Barbara Lorey De Lacharrière, Philip Madanire, Jackie
McAllister, Jacqueline Milliet, Stéphane de Montmollin,
Aaron Mullan, Sophia Murer, Ellen B. Napier, Françoise
Ninghetto, Eveline Notter, Carmen Pennella, Ben
Pettinato, Eva Presenhuber, Annemarie Reichen,
Katrein Reist, Ambassador Jacques Reverdin, Markus
Rischgasser, Rosemarie Richner, Anne Roussel, Frank
Russek, Sandra Schafroth, Scipio Schneider, Kathy
Schindelheim, Melvin Smith, Patricia Schramm, Eveline
Steinmann, Ali Subotnick, Daniel Tierney, Matt Tierney,
Rudolf Velhagen, Antoine Vigne, Martina Volpe, Suzanne
and Willy Wahler, Pierre-Alain Wahler, Beat von
Wartburg, Rachel K. Ward, Arthur Woods, Ivo Zanetti.

Marc-Olivier Wahler would like to extend his warm thanks
to Dieter von Graffenried, for his precious advice and
constant support, Fabienne Abrecht, for her great
energy and generosity, to Gabrielle Giattino, for her
efficiency, coolness, and intelligence, to Niklaus Thönen,
for his dedication, speed, and skills, and to the whole
S1 staff and board members.